HANDBOOK FOR THE
TEACHER OF SWIMMING

HANDBOOK
FOR TEACHER
THE
OF SWIMMING

Colin A. Hardy

PELHAM BOOKS
LONDON

First published in Great Britain by
Pelham Books Ltd
27 Wrights Lane
London W8 5TZ
1987

British Library Cataloguing in Publication Data

Hardy, Colin
Handbook for the teacher of swimming.
1. Swimming——Study and teaching
I. Title
797.2′1′07   GV836.35

ISBN 0-7207-1745-0

Typeset by Cambridge Photosetting Services

Printed in Great Britain by The Bath Press, Bath

The line drawings are by Ted Koehorst of
Vincent Design, Cambridge.

CONTENTS

FOREWORD

by David Moorcroft and Rick Bailey

The importance of Colin Hardy's book reflects the increase in the number of people, of all ages, who take part in this sport.

An increased awareness of the value of swimming as a form of exercise has meant that people need to learn not only how to swim but also how to swim well. This book gives all those involved in the learning process concise, clear and well presented points on the acquisition of the skills.

The growth in numbers of participants in other water based activities gives further reason to promote the teaching of swimming skills.

For those involved in the teaching of swimming at all levels, this book will become an invaluable reference and one that I am sure will contribute towards more people getting greater satisfaction from the sport.

> DAVID MOORCROFT
> *International Athlete;*
> *T.V. Commentator;*
> *Director of the Coventry and*
> *Warwickshire Awards Trust.*

This book presents a comprehensive and thorough approach to the preparation and implementation of sound teaching techniques as they apply to swimming.

The reader will find the chapter on swimming strokes uncomplicated and enhanced by the follow-up practices, which I feel sure will help in the achievement of instructional objectives for the swimming programme, whether it be in the school curriculum or within a swimming club context.

Skills often left out of the swimming syllabus through lack of confidence on the part of the teacher or insufficient resource material are well presented in the chapters on Elementary Diving and Starts and Turns. Here again the reader will find the concise presentation of teaching points and useful diagrams invaluable in overcoming some of the difficulties encountered by young people in skill acquisition.

Colin Hardy's attention to detail underlines the importance of careful lesson planning to achieve the desired results. At no time, however, will the reader feel confused by technical jargon and advanced theory. This is very much a practical book, one which I am certain will be more than just another reference work.

Swimming teachers, prospective students of swimming and those already well-qualified will find this *Handbook for the Teacher of Swimming* a useful ally in the presentation and evaluation of their swimming lessons. It is, without doubt, a very welcome addition to the swimming 'book-shelf' although I think it most unlikely that it will be very far from the pool side.

RICK BAILEY D.L.C.
ASA Senior Coach;
Swimming Management Officer,
City of Birmingham District Council;
Chief Coach, G.B. Olympic Swimming Team 1984.

This book is dedicated to my parents
for introducing me to the sport of swimming

Acknowledgements

I would like to thank my family for their help and support: my wife, Jennifer, for checking the manuscript; my elder daughter, Rebecca, for doing the original sketches for the illustrations; and my younger daughter, Charlotte, for trying out the practices. I would also like to thank Derek Blease for the photography, and Sue Johnson for typing the manuscript. A mention must be made of all those Loughborough students, both past and present, who have contributed to the ideas in this book.

1 PLANNING OF THE SWIMMING PROGRAMME

The planning of an effective swimming programme involves a detailed observation of pupils and requires a thorough knowledge of swimming techniques and an understanding of teaching strategies.

Teaching structures

Source unit

A source unit is a detailed outline of the content needed to teach a particular area of work. It usually includes the following information:

- i) Background of the activity
- ii) Nature of the activity
- iii) Terminology
- iv) Rules and regulations
- v) Safety precautions
- vi) Skills and teaching points
- vii) Teaching practices

The material in a source unit is usually the result of collating information gained from known texts, from professional courses and from the teacher's experience of the area.

Block unit

A block unit gives details of the course to be taught. It usually includes the following information:

- i) Name of teacher
- ii) Date and unit duration
- iii) Facilities and teaching aids
- iv) Methods and techniques
- v) Unit organization
- vi) Swimming programme goal, general instructional objectives and specific instructional objectives
- vii) Entry skills required

viii) Rules, regulations and safety precautions
ix) Skills and relevant teaching points
x) Practices
xi) Evaluation procedures

In preparing a block unit the details concerning the rules and regulations, the skills and teaching points can be extracted from the source unit.

The actual organization of the block unit may take many forms. The material may be organized starting with the simple and going on to the more difficult, or according to its use in the particular activity. The teacher could develop the work through group or individual assignments, or through competition practices. In some block units the pupil could be involved in the planning of the material. The pupil might just select from set assignments or he/she might actually have some say in the planning of the objectives. In organizing the block unit the swimming teacher must decide how best to use the subject matter in the interests of the pupil.

Lesson plan The lesson plan is a concise outline of the content to be taught to a class on a particular day and for a period of time. It usually includes the following information:

i) Details of the class
ii) Date and lesson duration
iii) Facilities and teaching aids
iv) Methods and techniques
v) Presentation and class organization
vi) Instructional sequence and time schedule
vii) General instructional objectives and specific instructional objectives
viii) Pupil pre-requisites
ix) Rules, regulations and safety precautions
x) Skills and relevant teaching points
xi) Practices
xii) Lesson evaluation

The lesson plan is a carefully structured document that the teacher uses to transmit subject matter to the child and to develop practical competences.

Swimming programme In planning the swimming programme the teacher must first resolve a number of issues (Fig. 1.1). The teacher must decide whether the course is going to be orientated more to the individual than to the group and whether the course is going to be teacher or pupil determined. It is not possible for a teacher to put *every* theoretical idea into practice, but it is possible to consider the problems and to go some way in bridging the gaps.

FIG. 1.1

PLANNING ISSUES

Width	*v.*	narrowness of programme
Individual	*v.*	group needs, interests and capabilities
Pupil	*v.*	teacher determined programmes
Individual	*v.*	team competition
Normal	*v.*	atypical child
Teacher capabilities	*v.*	ambitious programmes
Teacher ideals	*v.*	realistic conditions
Individual	*v.*	team teaching
Teaching	*v.*	coaching
Institutional	*v.*	community needs and interests
Institutional	*v.*	parental needs and interests
Choice	*v.*	no choice
Awards	*v.*	no awards
Competition	*v.*	co-operation
Age	*v.*	ability groups
Single sex	*v.*	mixed groups
Absolute	*v.*	relative success
Specialization in swimming	*v.*	integration with other curriculum subjects

Goals and instructional objectives

Goals indicate general outcomes of the school or community programme, whereas the instructional objectives are statements of the skills you hope a pupil will achieve after instruction.

Instructional objectives are frequently discussed at two levels, a general and a specific one. The general instructional objective gives direction to the teaching and testing of material in the block unit and the specific instructional objective indicates the learning outcome in precise and measurable terms for each lesson.

Examples of goals: i) Performs the competitive strokes
ii) Performs the non-competitive strokes
iii) Performs diving and turning skills

Examples of general instructional objectives: If the goal is *Performs the competitive strokes*, the general instructional objectives could include:

i) Swims the breaststroke in a technically correct way
ii) Swims the backcrawl in a technically correct way
iii) Swims the frontcrawl in a technically correct way
iv) Swims the butterfly dolphin in a technically correct way

Examples of specific instructional objectives: Specific instructional objectives for the general instructional objective *Swims the breaststroke in a technically correct way* could include:

i) Swims 25 metres breaststroke in an uncrowded lane demonstrating a simultaneous and symmetrical leg action
ii) Swims 25 metres breaststroke in an uncrowded lane demonstrating a simultaneous and symmetrical arm action
iii) Swims 25 metres breaststroke in an uncrowded lane demonstrating a circular leg kick with the feet turned outwards
iv) Swims 25 metres breaststroke in an uncrowded lane demonstrating a continuous arm pull and recovery movement

Monitoring progress and evaluation

Tests designed to show how well a pupil performs on given swimming tasks following instruction provide useful information on the pupil's progress. Such tests can be used to measure the control each pupil has over the skills in a particular swimming programme rather than to rank pupils.

The test items directly measure the achievement of the stated specific instructional objective, and, if the required number of test items are passed, the pupil proceeds to the next part of the work. The majority of pupils would be expected to proceed.

It is important that the test items are closely representative of the instructional content (content validity) and they appear to be valid tests by all (face validity). It would also be expected that the test items be administered under similar conditions for all pupils.

The directions (teacher to pupil) for the specific instructional objective *Swims 25 metres breaststroke in an*

Movement – Breaststroke   FIG. 1.2

Tick box if the item is completed successfully,   comment if necessary

i) Swims 25 metres in an uncrowded lane   ☑ *Stopped twice and held side for a moment*

ii) Swims 25 metres without stopping or   ☐ *should manage this next time.*
touching the side or bottom of the pool

iii) Leg action is simultaneous and symmetrical ☑ *Sound leg kick*

uncrowded lane demonstrating a simultaneous and sym-metrical leg action could read as follows:

Please swim breaststroke for one length of the pool in the end lane. The distance you will be swimming is 25 metres. To receive credit you must complete the length without stopping or touching the side or bottom of the pool, and you must demonstrate a simultaneous and symmetrical leg action. (Adapt language for younger children.)

Test items are then prepared (Fig. 1.2) to measure the pupil's achievement on the stated specific instructional objective.

Normally the test would be administered immediately after the instructional period, but there are reasons why it could be administered at other times. If a block unit has been planned and relevant tests have been prepared based on the specific instructional objectives, the teacher might decide to administer the test prior to the instructional programme. The results of such tests will indicate whether any of the required movements have already been achieved by the pupils and can be of value in organizing ability groups for the instruction to follow.

If the test is administered immediately after the instructional period, the results point the way to future activities for the pupil and they can be used as a basis for evaluation. In the latter case the teacher might decide that any child who achieves a certain number of the swimming stroke objectives throughout the year may be judged as a competent performer of the competitive strokes.

Sometimes a test is administered after a period of time has elapsed from the initial instruction. In this case the results may indicate the maintenance of a skill level which could be important in evaluating the effectiveness of the

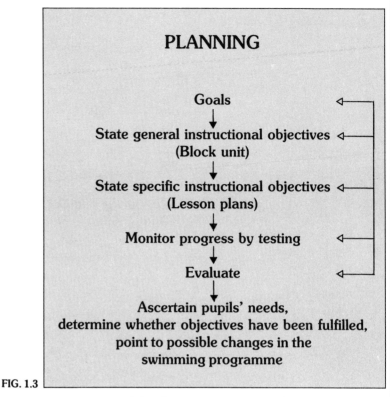

PLANNING

Goals

↓

State general instructional objectives
(Block unit)

↓

State specific instructional objectives
(Lesson plans)

↓

Monitor progress by testing

↓

Evaluate

↓

Ascertain pupils' needs,
determine whether objectives have been fulfilled,
point to possible changes in the
swimming programme

FIG. 1.3

instruction and for future programme development.

If, for various administrative or other reasons, the instructional time is curtailed, the teacher may decide not to use all the test items in monitoring progress. In the case of the breaststroke leg action objective the teacher may be satisfied if the pupil completes half the length correctly.

The teacher who monitors a pupil's progress by administering tests is not evaluating the performance. If a teacher judges a pupil's performance as *good* or *average* then it can be said that an evaluation has been made. The evaluation will not be based wholly on measurements taken but on the teacher's experience of other groups of pupils and an understanding of swimming content. Evaluation is a term that means more than measurement and helps the teacher to ascertain the needs of the pupils, to determine whether the objectives have been fulfilled and to point to areas of change in the swimming programme.

Methods of teaching swimming

In the present context the author is interpreting method as the way in which the pupil attempts a swimming skill. Although the teacher may vary the oral and visual techniques and may play a central or lesser role in directing and managing the pupils, there comes a time when part of or the whole skill must be attempted. The organization of these part and whole practices gives rise to four methods:

i) In the progressive-part method the pupil practises one part of a particular skill, then a second part, and then practises the two together. Parts are then added until the whole skill is reached. The pupil may practise the butterfly leg action, then the arm action, and then the pupil practises the arm and leg movements together over short distances and with no breathing action. The arm and breathing actions may then be taught and added to the leg movements.

ii) In the part-whole method the pupil learns parts of the skill first before attempting the whole skill. The teacher may decide that once the breaststroke leg action has been taught the pupil should attempt the complete stroke. It would not be necessary in this method to go through every individual part before attempting the whole skill.

iii) In the whole-part-whole method the pupil attempts the whole skill, then practices a part of the skill and finally goes back to the whole skill. For example, the pupil attempts the front-crawl, practises the leg kick separately, and then goes back to practising the full stroke. If the pupil has difficulty in performing the complete stroke a buoyancy aid could be used.

iv) In the whole method the pupil attempts to improve the skill by concentrating upon one aspect while performing the whole movement. The backstroker may concentrate upon the toes breaking the surface while performing the complete stroke. With this method it is necessary that the pupil can perform the skill with competence, but, once again, a buoyancy aid could be used to help the less competent pupil.

Pupil aids In the initial stages of learning to swim, costumes with pockets for polystyrene floats or inflatable arm, waist, barbell and ring floats are used to support the pupil above the surface, to achieve the horizontal position and to help the pupil to practise the swimming movements. Hand paddles are used to improve arm techniques, and polystyrene floats can be held by the hands or placed between the legs to improve leg and arm movements respectively.

One particular arrangement of equipment used in swimming is known as the flipper-float technique. A pupil, who wears fins and holds a float, is supported in the prone horizontal position by a rubber covered loop of rope suspended from a short pole held by the teacher. Once the pupil has achieved an effective leg kick, the teacher lowers the loop and allows the pupil to move unwittingly without this support. If the pupil assumes the horizontal supine position and holds the float on the abdomen the teacher can pass the loop under the pupil's neck and perform a similar manoeuvre.

A pace clock can be used to time specific practices such as treading water, a one hundred-metre swim, or to control pace during a swim.

Apparatus such as wall-bars, ropes, beams and benches, resistance exercise machines and weights are used to prepare more advanced swimmers for high level performances. A large mirror placed in an appropriate position on the poolside can aid pupils in perfecting swimming movements.

A shallow pool is a medium for teaching non-swimmers. The pool must be shallow enough for the pupil to place the hands on the bottom and to keep the head above the surface while assuming a prone or supine position. As the pupil begins to feel the support given by the water, effective arm and leg movements can be developed.

Teaching design

Once the teacher has established that the pupil is ready and willing to learn a particular skill the teacher prepares a teaching design. In preparing the design the teacher will have to decide whether to control the instructional procedures closely or whether to allow the pupil more freedom by giving individual and group assignments. The design will include suitable teaching methods, relevant verbal instruction and the use of visual aids. In the latter the teacher could use still pictures, charts, blackboard diagrams, video-tape recorders, slides, film loops and overhead projectors.

The common features of a lesson design are:

i)   Introduction: it is usual to introduce the lesson content indicating its relevance and importance to the swimming course. A well thought-out introduction can inspire an enthusiasm for the activity to follow.

ii) Demonstration/instruction: the teacher gives a clear

picture of the activity to be taught by combining visual and verbal techniques.

iii) Performance: the pupil practises the activity using a number of variations of individual, group and class drills.

iv) Summary: the teacher may re-emphasize the main points of the lesson and involve the pupil in discussion to determine the quality of the work and its use in future activities.

In introducing the lesson content to the pupils the teacher must ensure that they can see and hear (Fig. 1.4).

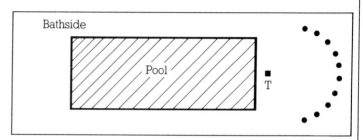

FIG. 1.4

The explanation should be concise and to the point, and the teacher should speak in a low pitched voice with varying inflection and clear enunciation. The explanation would usually take place on the pool side before pupils enter the water.

Example of an explanation: *You are going to learn how to get back to a starting position from gliding on your front. This is important for safety, so you know you can get your feet back on the bottom of the pool. You will have to use your head, arms and legs and the movement is rather like doing a through vault over a box.*

Example of an instruction for a demonstration: *If you are going to get your feet on the bottom of the pool from the front glide position, you must press down with your hands, lift your head and tuck up your knees. When you feel you are upright, straighten your legs.*

Once this specific detail has been given the main aspects of the skill are emphasized in the form of a teaching point. The teaching point should start with a verb, be easily understood by the pupil and, if carried out, should improve the pupil's performance.

In the text some teaching points may seem to overlap but this is intentional. Firstly, there may be several ways of stating the teaching point to achieve the same outcome. Secondly, when several movements are involved teaching points may refer to the whole skill and/or just part of it.

Examples of teaching points for regaining the feet from the prone position: *Press downwards with the hands, Lift the head, Tuck the legs.*

The instruction must now be given for the pupils to perform, and this can be done in the form of an instruction followed by a definite word of command.

Example of an instruction and command: *Enter the water and swim six widths* may be the direction to a well controlled group of pupils, whereas *Swim six widths frontcrawl . . . Go!* (or a clap of the hands or a whistle) may be more appropriate with the large class where control is sometimes difficult.

In the performance part of the activity the teacher can use a number of pupil formations depending upon the instructional content.

Examples of pupil formations:

i) One group at a time is sent to the opposite side of the bath in wave formation.

ii) Individual pupils leave the side one at a time in cannon (or stagger) formation.

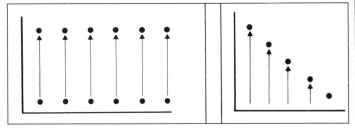

FIG. 1.5

FIG. 1.6

iii) The pupils go backwards and forwards remaining in the same lane.

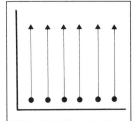

FIG. 1.7

iv) The pupils perform slow or stationary movements in an open space formation.

Shallow end

Deep water

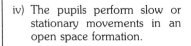

FIG. 1.8

v) The pupils perform the movements in a circular path.

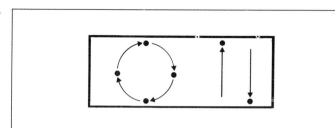

FIG. 1.9

Examples of teacher positioning:

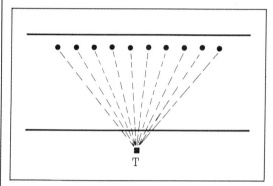

FIG. 1.10

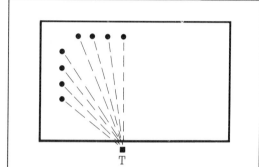

FIG. 1.11

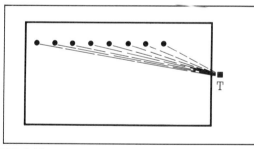

FIG. 1.12

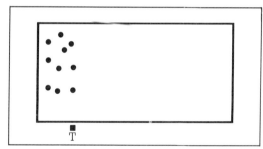

FIG. 1.13

Examples of teaching designs: A large group of pupils learning breaststroke arm action for the first time.

i)
- a) Introduction
- b) Demonstration/instruction
- c) Class practice: pupils imitate the teacher's performance of the breaststroke arm movement and then perform the movement from memory
- d) Individual or group practices: pupils perform a set number of breaststroke arm and full stroke practices in their own time
- e) Class practice: pupils perform breaststroke arm practices sometimes imitating the teacher's performance

and sometimes from memory

   f)   Summary

ii)   A large group of pupils of mixed ability improving breaststroke arm action.

   a)   Group positions based on ability levels

   b)   Introduction

   c)   Demonstration/instruction

   d)   Group practices controlled by the teacher: pupils perform the appropriate breaststroke arm and full stroke practices in their ability groups

   e)   Summary

iii)   A class of advanced pupils improving different swimming strokes.

   a)   Introduction

   b)   Demonstration/instruction

   c)   Group instructions: instructions giving details of the practices and the main teaching points are written on appropriate materials and placed conveniently for each group to see

   d)   Group practices

   e)   Summary

2 THE SWIMMING STROKES

Background

It is probable that in the past a form of dog-paddle was the most widely performed action, although there is evidence to suggest that an overarm stroke was used in antiquity.

At the beginning of the nineteenth century the breast-stroke was commonly used and was the fastest stroke, but it was later replaced by underarm and overarm side-strokes. Towards the end of the century John Trudgeon combined a scissors kick with an alternating overarm action.

In the development of backstroke-swimming the breaststroke leg kick was combined with a simultaneous movement of the arms. The arms were recovered under-arm to a position beyond the head and then pulled to the sides of the body. Later, the arms were recovered alternately and over the water surface.

The frontcrawl stroke was introduced in about 1900, and this was soon followed by the development of the backcrawl stroke. The butterfly breaststroke was intro-duced in the 1930s and by the 1950s the butterfly dolphin was in general use. As the four competitive strokes were improved, so were the appropriate starting and turning techniques.

Breaststroke

BODY POSITION

All swimmers should be as near horizontal as possible, although the advanced swimmer should make a more conscious effort to streamline the leg, arm and breathing movements.

LEGS

Once the legs are straight and the toes pointed, the heels are brought up to the seat. With the learner the knees move forwards and outwards with the heels close together; with the advanced swimmer the knees are closer together and the trunk-thigh angle is approxi-mately 110 degrees. The feet are then dorsi-flexed and turned outwards, and the kick is outwards, backwards and then together. The toes are extended as the legs straighten and move towards each other. The advanced swimmer tends to kick more vigorously backwards, and the feet perform a whip-like movement in a more narrowly curved path.

The propulsion is obtained from the drive backwards with the inner surfaces of the feet and lower legs pressing against the water.

ARMS When the arms have been extended in front of the body and under the water, the palms are turned partly outwards and the eyes are directed downwards and forwards. The hands are pulled sideways, backwards and downwards to a position in front of the shoulder line. The elbows are then bent, and the hands move inwards and then immediately forwards; the palms face downwards and partly inwards during the recovery. The learner keeps the arms straight during the pull stage, but the advanced swimmer increasingly bends at the elbow and inwardly rotates the arms once the hands are about shoulder-width apart to ensure that the elbows remain high ('high elbow' technique) as the hands move backwards and inwards.

BREATHING The learner tends to inhale during the arm pull, whereas the advanced swimmer inhales at the end of the arm pull. The learner exhales as the arms stretch forwards and the advanced swimmer exhales, with increasing force, during the arm pull. The inhalation is taken through the mouth and the exhalation is made through the mouth and nose. All children should be encouraged to lift their chins forwards and upwards to inhale, rather than lift their heads, and to breathe in once every arm cycle. The face is submerged before the arms are fully stretched.

TIMING The learner pulls and inhales, recovers the arms and legs and kicks as the arms move forwards. With the advanced swimmer the legs start to recover towards the end of the pull and the kick begins before the arms have been fully extended in front of the body; final arm extension is reached as the kick is near completion.

TEACHING POINTS – BREASTSTROKE

Body position (prone and non-inhalation position)

a) look forwards and downwards

b) keep the head steady

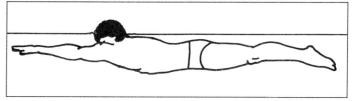

Legs (recovery)

STARTING POSITION:

the legs and ankles are stretched and together

a) bring the heels up to the seat

b) move the knees forwards and outwards

c) bring the heels closer together

d) cock and turn the feet outwards before the kick

e) bring the toes to the shins

f) keep the knees close together and high (advanced swimmer)

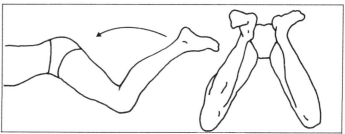

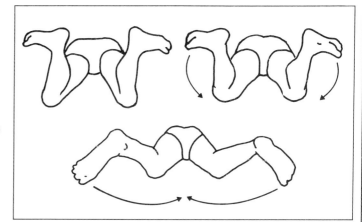

Legs (kick)

a) kick outwards, backwards and together

b) describe a circle with the feet

c) sweep the legs round and together

d) straighten the legs and the ankles during the kick

e) kick like a frog

f) press backwards with the inner surfaces of the feet and the lower legs

g) thrust the water backwards with the soles of the feet

h) kick and wait

i) kick backwards and together (advanced swimmer)

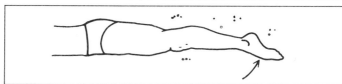

Arms (pull)

STARTING POSITION:

the arms are extended in front of the body and beneath the water surface

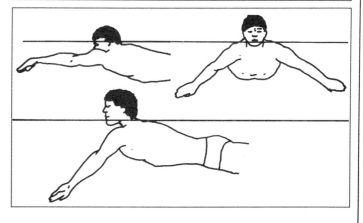

a) pull sideways, backwards and downwards
b) keep the arms straight
c) keep the wrists firm during the pull
d) keep the hands in sight
e) keep the hands in front of the shoulders
f) press down and out and start to bend (advanced swimmer)
g) increase the elbow bend as the arms press outwards (advanced swimmer)
h) press and bend (advanced swimmer)
i) keep the elbows up (advanced swimmer)
j) pull with increasing speed (advanced swimmer)

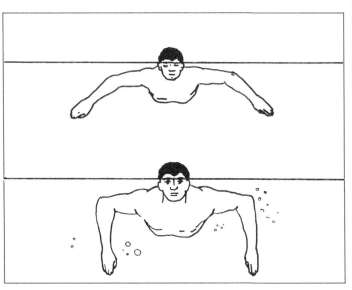

Arms (recovery)
a) bend at the elbows and bring the backs of the hands under the chin
b) bend the arms and bring the hands to the chin
c) stretch the arms forwards
d) swirl the hands together and immediately forwards (advanced swimmer)
e) swirl the elbows inwards and immediately forwards (advanced swimmer)

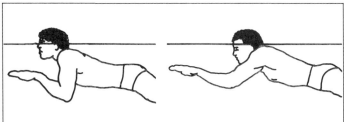

Arms (general)
a) keep the arms under the water surface
b) perform a heart-shaped pattern with the hands (advanced swimmer)

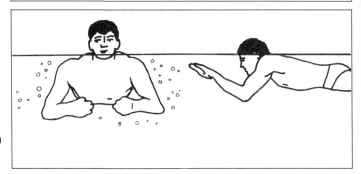

Breathing
a) breathe in during the pull
b) breathe out as the arms stretch forwards

(OPPOSITE) BREASTSTROKE: keep the wrists firm during the pull.

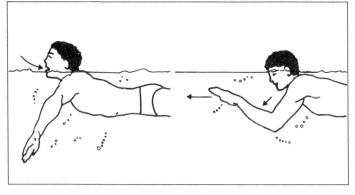

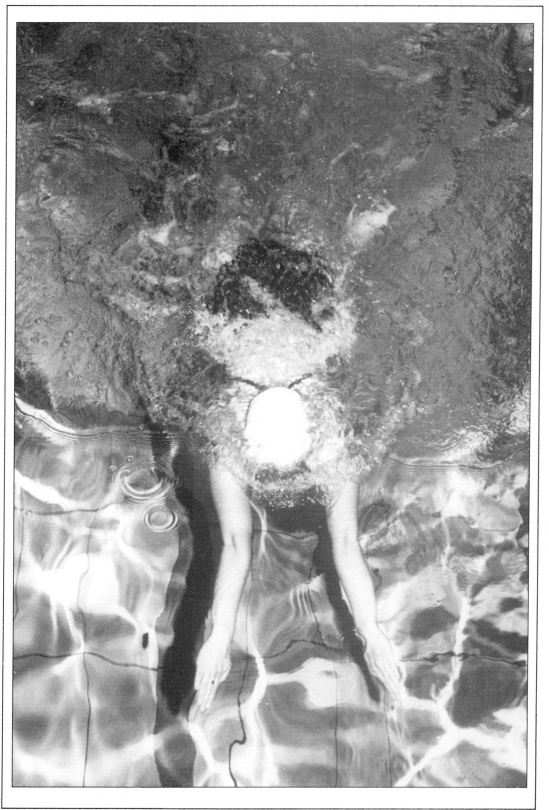

c) push the chin forwards to breathe

d) pull and breathe out and in (explosive breathing)

e) breathe out as the pull begins (advanced swimmer)

f) breathe in at the end of the pull (advanced swimmer)

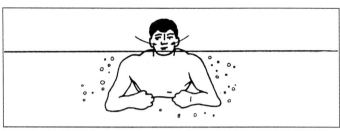

Timing

a) pull, recover the arms and the legs

b) kick as the arms stretch forwards

c) pull, recover, stretch and kick

d) breathe in and pull, breathe out and kick

e) start the leg recovery before the end of the pull (advanced swimmer)

f) thrust the arms forwards and then kick (advanced swimmer)

g) extend the arms and complete the kick (advanced swimmer)

h) start pull and breathe out, complete pull, breathe in and kick (advanced swimmer)

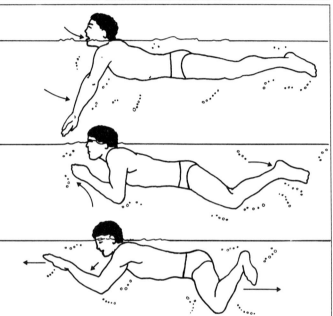

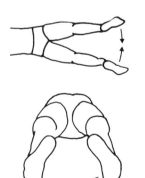

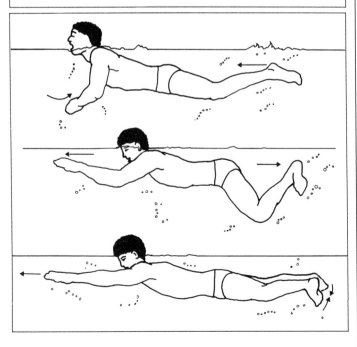

Backcrawl

BODY POSITION

The body is in a near horizontal supine position with the hips just below the water surface. The head is almost in line with the body with the water breaking the head around the ears. The downward movement of the hand at the end of the 'S' pull will create some body roll.

LEGS

The kick is hip initiated with the legs moving alternately, close together, continuously and mainly in the vertical plane. The leg moves downwards in an extended position, bends near the bottom of the movement and extends vigorously on the upbeat. The foot is well extended and in-toed on the upward movement and will churn the water close to the surface. The foot will go no deeper than forty-five centimetres at the end of the downbeat. The knee should remain just below the water surface throughout the leg action.

ARMS

The arm enters the water in an extended position beyond the head and in line with the shoulder. The hand enters with the palm outwards and sinks to a depth of fifteen to thirty centimetres. The beginner's pull is a shallow, sideways movement to the hips. The arm recovers in an upward and forward movement with the palm facing inwards.

As the arm passes the vertical, the hand is turned outwards in preparation for the entry. The arm action is a continuous movement with one arm pulling as the other is recovered.

The advanced swimmer's pull starts with a straight arm, but the elbow begins to bend and the arm inwardly rotates and adducts as the hand moves backwards. The pull is known as the 'S' pull because of the up and down path the hand traces, and will probably have to be specifically taught.

BREATHING

It is suggested that the swimmer inhales when it is convenient or when the need is felt. However, to avoid shallow breathing, it may be more beneficial to urge children to breathe in a regular pattern. Inhale through the mouth as one arm recovers and exhale through the mouth and nose as the other arm recovers.

TIMING

With the majority of swimmers and learners the timing is six leg beats to one complete arm cycle, and while one arm is pulling the other is recovering.

TEACHING POINTS – BACKCRAWL

Body position (supine)

a) get the ears under the surface
b) look upwards
c) keep the head still
d) keep the hips up

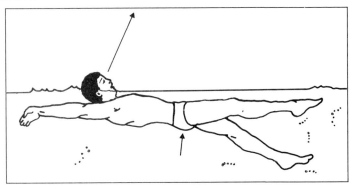

Legs

STARTING POSITION:
one leg is straight and near the surface and the other leg is bent with the foot at a depth of 30 to 45 centimetres

a) kick from the hips
b) kick the legs alternately up and down
c) keep the legs close together as they pass each other
d) stretch the toes
e) turn the toes inwards
f) kick the feet off
g) kick up and down continuously
h) churn the water near the surface
i) keep the knees below the surface
j) kick down with a straight leg
k) bend the leg at the bottom of the kick
l) straighten the leg at the top of the kick
m) press the instep against the water on the upward movement

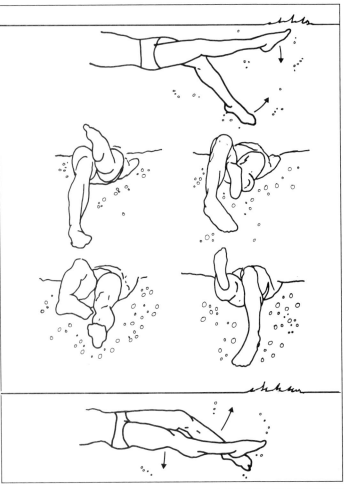

Arms (entry and pull)

STARTING POSITION:
one arm is straight and beyond the head

a) enter with the arm straight

(OPPOSITE) *BACKCRAWL: pull and bend the arm (advanced swimmer).*

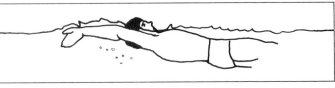

b) enter above the shoulder
c) enter with the palm outwards
d) enter with the little finger first
e) sink and pull to the side
f) pull sideways with a straight arm
g) keep the arm just under the surface
h) keep the wrist firm
i) keep the fingers closed
j) pull to the hip
k) pull and push down the body (advanced swimmer)
l) pull and bend the arm (advanced swimmer)
m) bend until the shoulder is reached (advanced swimmer)
n) push backwards and downwards (advanced swimmer)
o) keep the hand parallel to the body (advanced swimmer)
p) keep the palm facing backwards towards the feet (advanced swimmer)
q) turn the body into the pulling arm (advanced swimmer)
r) let the hand lead the pull (advanced swimmer)
s) pull with increasing speed (advanced swimmer)

Arms (recovery)

STARTING POSITION:
one arm is straight and by the side of the body
a) lift the hand out of the water with the thumb leading
b) lift the hand up and back
c) lift the hand up and place beyond the head
d) keep the arm straight
e) turn the palm outwards

f) reach backwards with the fingers

Breathing

a) breathe in as one arm recovers and breathe out as the other arm recovers

Timing

a) pull with one arm and recover with the other
b) keep the arms moving
c) kick hard as the arms pull and recover
d) kick and keep the arms moving

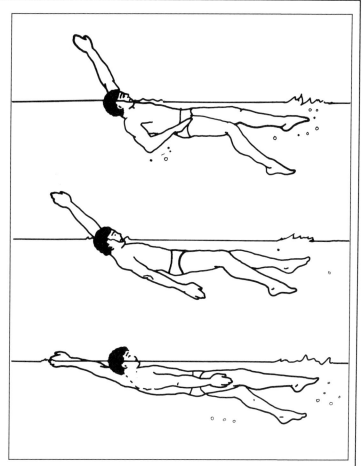

Frontcrawl

BODY POSITION

This is probably the most horizontal of all strokes. The swimmer looks forwards and downwards, breaking the water with the top of the forehead. The hips are close to the water surface and there is some body roll.

LEGS

The kick is a hip-initiated movement with the legs moving alternately and continuously up and down. In general, the leg remains straight during the upbeat, partially bends at the top of the movement, and then straightens on the downbeat. The feet are turned slightly inwards and the ankles need to be extended, particularly on the downward movement so that the instep presses against the water in a backward and downward direction. The legs pass each other closely, and go to an approximate depth of thirty centimetres; the heels should just break the water surface.

ARMS The partly turned-out hand of the almost extended arm enters the water between the centre and shoulder line. As the hand begins to move backwards, the arm inwardly rotates and the elbow increasingly bends; the elbow remains high during the first part of the pull. As the hand passes the shoulder, it pushes backwards, outwards and towards the hip, and the arm almost completely straightens. The wrist should remain firm throughout the pull with the fingers together. The palm will be turned inwards just prior to the recovery.

In the recovery, the elbow increasingly bends as the arm swings upwards and forwards. The hand trails and the palm faces backwards and slightly upwards. On passing the shoulder, the hand leads the recovery in preparation for the entry. During the recovery the hand should be kept below the elbow, close to the body and close to the water surface. The degree of elbow bend during the propulsive and recovery phases of the arm varies according to the individual.

BREATHING The swimmer inhales when one arm is forwards and about to pull and the other arm is just leaving the water. The head is turned (not lifted) to the opposite side to the forward arm and the inhalation is made through the mouth. Exhalation takes place through the mouth and nose when the face is beneath the water surface. Breathing normally takes place once every arm cycle, but a bi-lateral technique (every third arm pull) can be used.

TIMING Six beats to one arm cycle is the common timing, but there are a number of very successful swimmers with a two beat co-ordination. Variations in leg kick will often depend on the racing distance and the arm strength of the swimmer.

TEACHING POINTS – FRONTCRAWL

Body position (prone and non-inhalation position)

a) break the water surface with the forehead
b) look downwards and slightly forwards
c) keep the hips up

Legs

STARTING POSITION:
one leg is slightly bent and

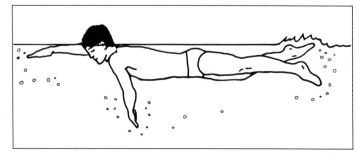

near the water surface and the other leg is straight with the foot at a depth of approximately 30 centimetres

a) kick from the hips
b) keep the knees almost straight
c) kick the legs alternately up and down
d) keep the legs close together
e) kick up and down continuously
f) turn the toes inwards
g) point the feet
h) bend the leg at the top of the kick
i) straighten the leg at the bottom of the kick
j) press the instep against the water on the downward beat

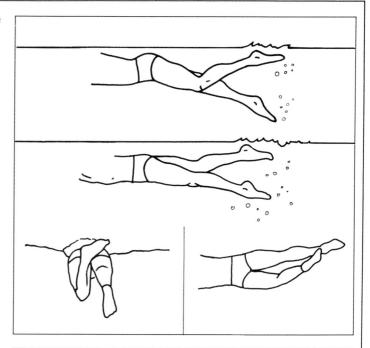

Arms (entry and pull)

STARTING POSITION:

one arm is almost straight and beyond the head

a) enter the water beyond the head
b) enter with the palm turned partly outwards
c) enter with the thumb first
d) enter the arm between the shoulder and the centre line
e) turn the palm downwards after entry
f) pull the hand back to the hips
g) bend the arm until beneath the shoulder
h) straighten the arm to the hips
i) pull and bend the arm
j) pull and keep the elbow up
k) push and straighten the arm
l) lead the pull and push with the hand

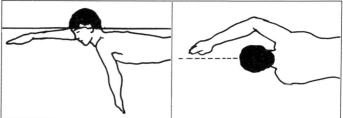

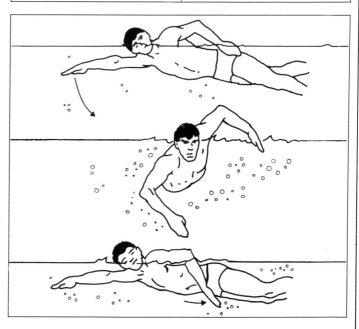

m) push to below the hips
n) keep the fingers closed
o) keep the palm facing
   backwards
p) keep the wrist firm
q) pull with increasing speed
   (advanced swimmer)

Arms (recovery)

STARTING POSITION:
one arm is almost straight by
the side of the body
a) lift the elbow out of the
   water first

(RIGHT AND BELOW) *FRONTCRAWL
– ARM RECOVERY: lift the elbow
and trail the hand.*

b) lift and bend the arm

c) swing the elbow upwards and forwards

d) lift the elbow and trail the hand

e) trail the hand with the palm facing backwards and upwards

f) keep the hand close to the water surface

g) lead the second half of the recovery with the hand

h) reach forwards with the hand

i) reach forwards and turn the palm downwards and outwards

j) lift the elbow up and stretch the hand forwards

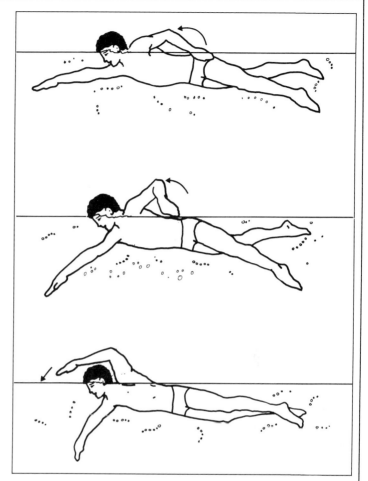

Breathing

a) breathe in as the hand on the breathing side completes the pull

b) breathe in through the mouth

c) turn the face to the side and breathe in

d) breathe out when the face is submerged

e) blow out through the mouth and nose

f) keep the ear near to the leading arm when turning to breathe in

g) turn, blow out and breathe in (explosive breathing)

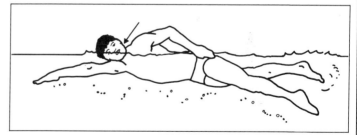

Timing

a) pull with one arm and recover with the other

b) keep the arms moving

c) kick as the arms pull and recover

d) kick and keep the arms moving

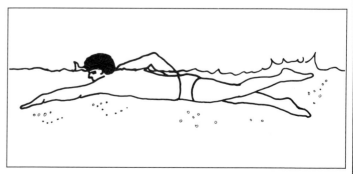

Butterfly dolphin

BODY POSITION

The body is as near horizontal as possible, but because of the powerful leg beat there is some undulation of the body. The hips remain close to the water surface, and the swimmer looks downwards and slightly forwards.

LEGS

In general the leg kick is similar to that of the frontcrawl except that the legs work together. The kick is hip-initiated, it is continuous and in the vertical plane. The upbeat is with extended legs; the legs partly bend at the top of the kick and vigorously straighten on the down-beat. The toes are pointed and the feet well stretched on the downbeat so that the instep and front of the leg are able to press against the water. With the learner it may be necessary to emphasize a shallow leg kick initiated from the knees because of the excessive body undulation that may occur with too great a hip movement.

ARMS

The hands enter the water with the palms facing outwards and downwards and with the elbows almost straight. The hands enter the water about shoulder-width apart, and then press downwards, outwards and backwards. During the first part of the pull, the arms start to bend and inwardly rotate, and a 'high elbow' technique is maintained. The hands tend to move towards each other in a curved path, and a maximum arm bend of approximately a right angle is reached at the half-way stage. The thumbs come close together as the hands are pushed backwards and the elbows straightened. The butterfly pull is sometimes called the hourglass pull because of the shape the hands make beneath the water surface. The palms turn inwards as the hands are lifted clear of the water. The arms now swing forwards in a low circular path with the hands trailing. As the arms move past the shoulders, the palms start to turn downwards in preparation for the entry.

BREATHING

The inhalation takes place through the mouth at the highest point of the stroke, which is at the end of the pull. Exhalation takes place with increasing force through the mouth and nose during the pull. The head is gradually raised during the pull so that the mouth comes clear of the water at the end. Once the inhalation has taken place the face is placed once more under the water. It is possible that a learner may adjust the arm action so that the pull is used more for lifting the head clear for breathing than for propulsion. In such circumstances the inhalation may take place earlier in the pull. The breathing rhythm can be performed every one or two arm cycles.

TIMING   Two legs beats to a continuous arm cycle is the common timing; the first downbeat comes as the arms are about to pull and the second downbeat comes towards the end of the pull. The young learner may be taught to use a three to four leg beat with a gliding arm action, but the strong teenager or adult learner may find a continuous arm action with a single leg beat easier.

TEACHING POINTS – BUTTERFLY DOLPHIN

Body position (prone and non-inhalation position)

a) break the water surface with the top of the forehead
b) look downwards and slightly forwards
c) keep the hips up

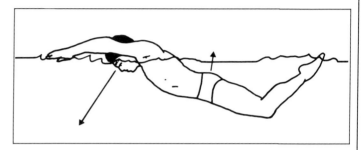

Legs

STARTING POSITION
at the completion of the upbeat the legs are together, slightly bent, with the toes pointed backwards; at the completion of the downbeat the legs are together and straight, with the ankles stretched

a) kick from the hips
b) keep the legs together
c) turn the feet slightly inwards
d) kick up and down continuously
e) kick up with the legs straight
f) bend the knees near the top of the upbeat
g) straighten the knees on the downbeat
h) press with the insteps and shins on the downbeat
i) stretch the toes on the downbeat

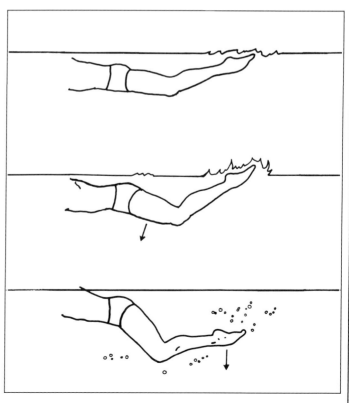

j) press with the soles of the feet on the upbeat

k) bend and straighten at the knees (beginner)

l) kick up and down from the knees (beginner)

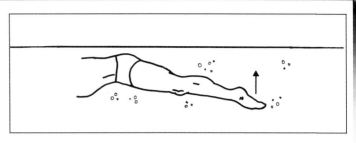

Arms (entry and pull)

STARTING POSITION:

the arms are extended beyond the head and just wide of the shoulder line with the palms facing partly downwards and outwards

a) enter the water beyond the head

b) enter with almost straight arms

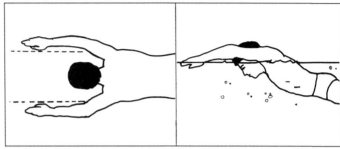

c) enter with the palms facing outwards and downwards

d) enter with the thumbs first

e) enter the hands just wide of the shoulders

f) press outwards and downwards

g) pull the hands outwards, backwards and inwards

h) make an hour-glass shape with the hands

i) bring the thumbs close together beneath the chest

j) pull inwards and push backwards and outwards

k) pull over the barrel

l) bend the arms to the shoulders and straighten to the thighs

m) pull and keep the elbows up

n) push backwards and stretch

o) push backwards with the palms

p) push and straighten the elbows

q) keep the wrists firm

r) keep the fingers closed

s) lead the 'pull and push' with the hands

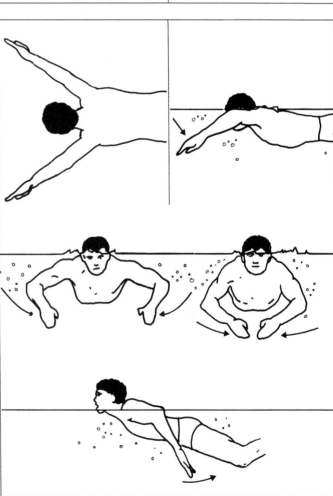

t) push backwards, outwards
    and upwards
u) pull with increasing speed
    (advanced swimmer)

Arms (recovery)

STARTING POSITION:
the arms are almost straight
by the sides of the body with
the elbows higher than the
hands

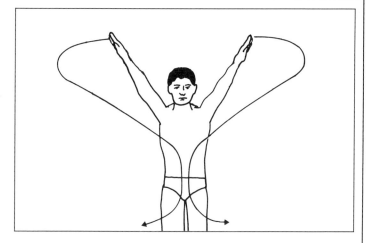

(RIGHT) *BUTTERFLY – ARM
RECOVERY: swing the arms
forward in a circular path.*

a) turn the palms inwards and lift out of the water
b) lift the slightly bent arms out of the water
c) swing the straight arms forwards over the water surface
d) swing the arms forwards in a low circular path
e) swing the arms forwards with the hands trailing
f) recover and turn the palms downwards
g) lower the face and recover the arms

Breathing

a) breathe in at the end of the pull
b) breathe out with increasing force during the pull
c) push the chin forwards to breathe in
d) extend the neck to breathe in
e) breathe out through the mouth and nose
f) look forwards and breathe in
g) breathe in and keep the chin on the water surface
h) pull and breathe out and in (explosive breathing)

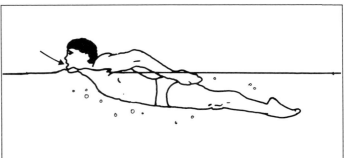

Timing

a) kick downwards as the hands enter the water (1st beat)
b) kick downwards as the hands push backwards (2nd beat)
c) kick downwards during the second half of the pull (2nd beat)
d) kick and then pull and recover the arms (beginners)
e) kick, pull, recover, glide (beginners)

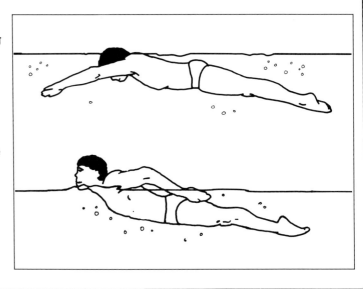

Sidestroke

BODY POSITION

The body is streamlined, lying on the side, face resting in the water. The head is turned to bring the chin towards the upper shoulder (facilitates breathing), and the lower arm is extended beyond the head with the palm downwards and under the water. The upper arm is extended along the body and is resting on the front side of the upper leg. The upper leg is resting over the lower leg and both legs are stretched with the toes pointed. There is a slight downward slope of the body from the head to the toes.

LEGS

From the side gliding position the legs are bent at the hips and knees and the heels are brought towards the hips. The legs are then spread gently into a striding position – the knees are kept bent as the upper leg moves forwards and the lower leg backwards. The toes of the upper leg will be pointing forwards and the toes of the lower leg backwards. In the propulsive phase the legs kick backwards and together in a scissors movement and straighten in the process. During the kick, pressure on the upper leg should be felt on the sole of the foot and the back of the leg, and on the lower leg it should be felt on the instep and the front of the leg. Once the legs are stretched and together with the toes pointed, there will be a pause. All leg movements should be made as near parallel to the water surface as possible.

In the reverse scissors kick the movement is identical to the regular movement except that the upper leg recovers backwards and kicks forwards, and the lower leg recovers forwards and kicks backwards.

ARMS

From the side gliding position the lower and leading arm increasingly bends as it is pulled downwards and backwards, and the upper and trailing arm is gradually bent as it is brought upwards towards the chin. The upper arm meets and then passes just above the lower arm to a point near to the opposite shoulder and close to the head. The upper arm with flexed wrist is pushed backwards towards the thigh, and the lower arm is stretched forwards beyond the head.

In the overarm sidestroke a bent upper arm is recovered over the water surface.

BREATHING

Inhalation takes place through the mouth as the lower arm pulls, and exhalation occurs through the mouth and nose as the lower arm recovers and glides.

TIMING The stroke begins with the pull of the lower and leading arm and it continues with the upper and trailing arm recovering as the heels are brought towards the hips. Once the two hands have passed each other and the legs are spread, the upper arm pulls and pushes, the lower arm stretches forwards beyond the head and the legs squeeze together. There is a short glide in the side gliding position.

TEACHING POINTS – SIDESTROKE

Body position (side)

a) lie on the side
b) look sideways and backwards
c) keep the side of the face in the water
d) keep the chin in
e) keep the chin near to the top shoulder

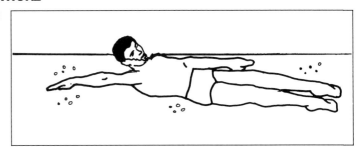

Legs (recovery)

STARTING POSITION:
the legs and ankles are stretched and together with the top leg resting on the bottom leg
a) bend and separate the legs
b) place the legs astride
c) spread the legs
d) move the top leg forwards (orthodox kick)
e) move the bottom leg backwards (orthodox kick)
f) point the toes of the top foot forwards
g) cock the top foot
h) point the toes of the bottom foot backwards
(in the reverse kick recovery the top leg is moved backwards and the bottom leg forwards)

Legs (kick)

a) scissor the legs
b) sweep the legs together
c) scissor and straighten the legs

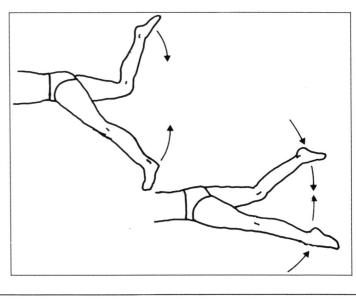

d) squeeze the legs together
e) thrust the feet together

Arms (pull and recovery)

STARTING POSITION:
the leading and bottom arm is stretched forwards, the top and trailing arm is stretched along the upper side of the body (side gliding position)

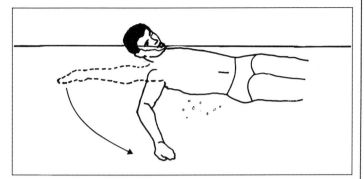

BOTTOM ARM:
a) pull the arm backwards
b) pull the arm towards the chin
c) pull by bending the arm
d) keep the elbow up
e) pull and then stretch the arm forwards
f) stretch the arm forwards beyond the head

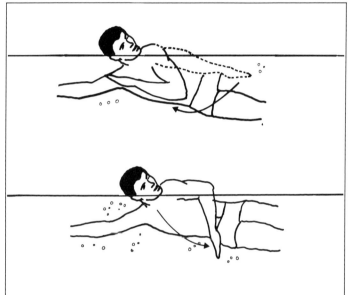

TOP ARM:
g) recover the arm towards the chin
h) recover and bend the arm close to the body
i) keep the elbow in
j) keep the elbow close to the chest
k) keep the palm of the hand downwards
l) keep the elbow submerged
m) keep the shoulder low
n) bring the hand in front of the face
o) push the hand backwards
p) press the hand downwards and backwards
q) push the arm to the hip
r) push backwards to the thigh

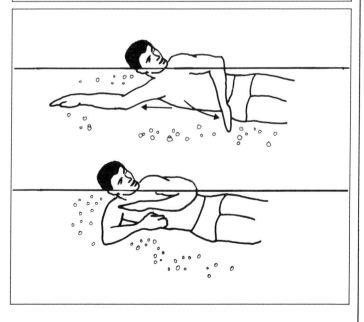

Arms (timing)

a) recover the top arm and pull the bottom arm
b) bring the hands inwards
c) bring the hands together

d) place the hands below the chin
e) keep the upper hand on top
f) push the top arm and stretch the bottom arm
g) move the hands outwards
h) stretch the arms
i) part the hands

Breathing

a) pull the bottom arm and breathe in
b) bring the hands inwards and breathe in
c) breathe in and bring the hands together
d) stretch the bottom arm and breathe out
e) move the hands outwards and breathe out
f) breathe out and stretch the arms
g) breathe out and part the arms
h) breathe in through the mouth
i) breathe out through the mouth and nose

Timing

a) bring the hands together and spread the legs
b) bend the arms and legs
c) part the hands and kick
d) straighten the arms and legs
e) stretch and glide
f) glide on the side

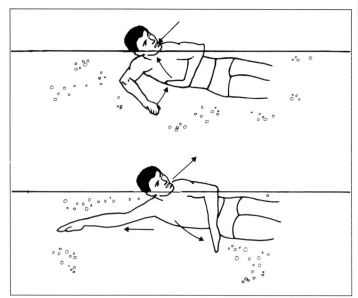

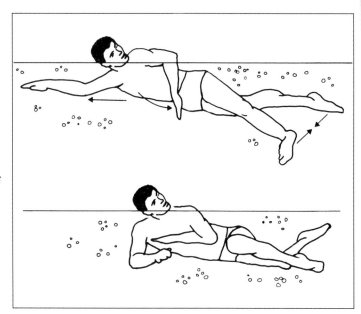

Elementary backstroke

BODY POSITION

The body is in a near horizontal supine position with the hips and legs slightly lowered to allow the legs to kick beneath the surface. The ears are submerged and the eyes are directed upwards. The arms are at the sides and the legs are together.

LEGS

The inverted breaststroke whip or wedge kick can be used in this stroke. In the whip kick recovery the knees are bent and the heels are dropped downwards and backwards towards the seat. The upper part of the legs should remain below and close to the water surface. The knees are spread but the feet stay close together. In preparation for the drive the feet are turned outwards and cocked as they approach the seat. During the leg drive the feet describe a semi-circular pattern as they move backwards, slightly outwards, towards the surface and together. The inside borders of the feet and ankles push against the water. The feet are vigorously straightened towards the end of the kick, and the legs are extended just prior to the feet coming together.

In the wedge kick the legs bend and turn outwards as the knees spread sideways and slightly upwards. The heels are kept close together and the knees stay just below the surface. With the toes turned towards the front of the lower legs (dorsi-flexed), the feet lead the leg drive in an outward, backward and inward movement. The legs straighten during this movement and come together with a final pointing of the toes.

ARMS From a position where the arms are at the sides, the elbows are bent downwards and outwards as the palms are drawn upwards along the sides of the body. The palms turn outwards as the hands approach the shoulders, and the elbows are brought close to the sides of the body. The elbows are pointing towards the feet. The arms are now straightened diagonally beyond the head ensuring that the arms remain beneath the water surface. With the elbows straight the arms are pulled forcefully downwards towards the feet. The pull is a shallow movement and is almost parallel to the water surface.

BREATHING Inhalation takes place through the mouth during the recovery of the arms and legs, and exhalation through the mouth and nose during the propulsive phase and glide.

TIMING With the arms at the sides and the legs together, the arms and legs are recovered at the same time. By the time the arms have straightened diagonally beyond the head the feet are about to drive. The kick and the pull are made simultaneously and a short glide is held before the next stroke starts. With the whip kick the leg drive finishes before the pull is completed.

TEACHING POINTS – ELEMENTARY BACKSTROKE

Body position (supine)
a) put the ears in the water
b) look upwards

Whip kick legs (recovery)
STARTING POSITION:
the legs and the ankles are stretched and together just below the water surface
a) drop the heels
b) bring the heels towards the seat
c) drop the heels downwards and backwards
d) keep the upper legs close to the surface
e) keep the feet close together
f) keep the knees under the surface
g) cock the feet
h) turn the feet outwards
k) cock and turn the feet outwards before the kick

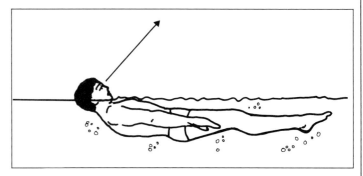

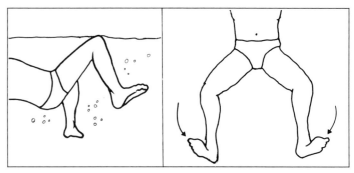

Whip kick legs (kick)
a) circle the lower legs
b) sweep the lower legs round and together
c) kick outwards and backwards
d) kick towards the surface
e) sweep the feet wide of the knees

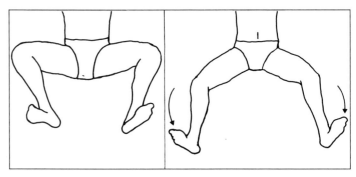

g) straighten and bring the legs together
h) keep the knees under the surface
i) push with the inside of the feet
j) kick and stretch the toes

Wedge kick legs (recovery)
STARTING POSITION:
the legs and the ankles are stretched and together just below the water surface

a) bring the heels towards the seat
b) bend the legs and spread the knees
c) spread the knees
d) move the knees sideways
e) keep the knees below the surface
f) keep the heels close together
g) cock the feet
h) turn the feet outwards
i) cock and turn the feet

outwards before the kick

Wedge kick legs (kick)
a) kick outwards and backwards
b) kick and straighten the legs
c) straighten and bring the legs together
d) keep the knees under the surface
e) push with inside of the feet
f) kick and stretch the toes

Arms (recovery)

STARTING POSITION:

the arms are straight at the sides of the body in the glide position

a) bend the arms
b) slide the palms upwards along the body
c) keep the palms downwards
d) point the elbows downwards and outwards
e) turn the palms outwards before stretching
f) keep the upper arms close to the body
g) bend and stretch the arms
h) stretch the arms outwards and forwards
i) stretch the arms beyond the head
j) stretch and make a V shape beyond the head
k) keep the arms under the surface
l) keep the palms outwards

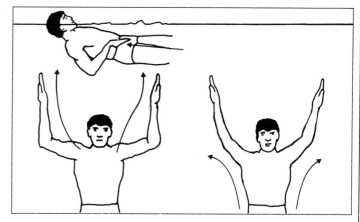

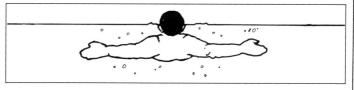

Arms (pull)

a) pull with straight arms
b) pull towards the feet
c) sweep the arms round
d) pull round to the sides
e) keep the arms below the surface
f) hold the arms by the sides
g) pull with increasing speed (advanced swimmer)

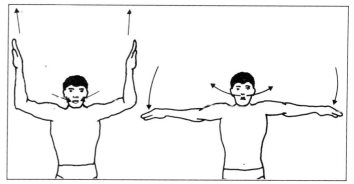

Breathing

a) breathe in and recover the arms
b) breathe in through the mouth
c) breathe out and pull
d) breathe out through the mouth and nose

Timing

a) recover the arms and legs
b) pull and kick

3 STROKE PRACTICES

Entry (shallow water)

NOTE: The following four alternative methods of entry into the pool may be useful to those pupils new to the water.

1. Walk down the steps slowly holding on to the rail or side. Stay close to the pool side.

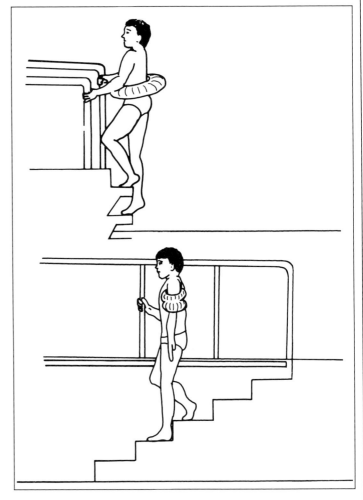

2. Walk down the steps slowly holding on to the hand of a partner who is already in the water.

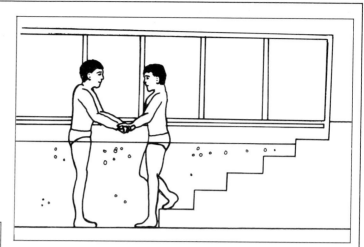

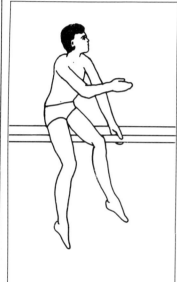

3. Sit on the pool side and take hold of the trough or rail with the palm of the hand facing towards the water. Drop into the water by pushing gently with the legs. Turn in towards the grasping hand as the body enters the water and grip the trough or rail in an overgrasp position with the other hand.

4. Stand in a semi-crouch or upright position and grip the toes round the edge of the pool side. Jump into the water towards a partner who helps to maintain balance once you have landed on the bottom of the pool.

Basic practices using the side, holding a float and with a partner

PRACTICE 1. Hold the side of the pool: raise the body and legs to a prone horizontal extended position and lower to place the feet on the bottom of the pool.

TEACHING POINTS

Hold

a) face the pool side
b) grasp over the rail (or trough)
c) bend the arms
d) keep the elbows against the wall   **or**

TOP HAND
a) grasp over the rail (or trough)
b) hold with a stretched but slightly bent arm

BOTTOM HAND
c) place the hand against the wall
d) place the hand underneath the top hand
e) point the fingers downwards
f) place the palm flat against the wall

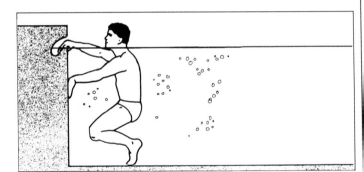

Raise the body

USING THE BENT ARM GRASP
a) force the elbows against the wall

PRONE HORIZONTAL & EXTENDED POSITION
b) stretch the legs
c) point the toes
d) look forwards

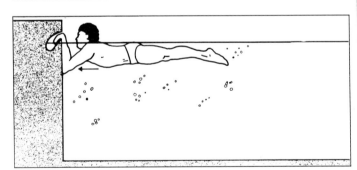

                or

USING THE SPLIT GRASP
a) push on the bottom arm
b) push against the wall

PRONE HORIZONTAL & EXTENDED POSITION
c) stretch the legs
d) point the toes
e) look forwards

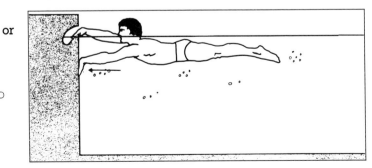

Lower the body

USING THE BENT ARM GRASP

a) pull the legs to the wall
b) tuck the legs
c) lift the head
d) lift the trunk

or

USING THE SPLIT GRASP

a) pull on the top arm
b) bend the top arm
c) pull inwards and upwards
d) pull the legs to the wall
e) tuck the legs
f) lift the head
g) lift the trunk

Stand

a) bring the legs under the body
b) stretch the legs downwards
c) release the arms

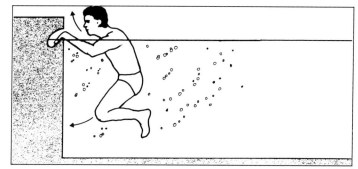
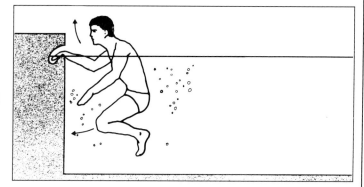

PRACTICE 2. Hold the side of the pool: raise the body and legs to a supine horizontal extended position and lower to place the feet on the bottom of the pool.

TEACHING POINTS

Hold

a) face outwards
b) grasp over the rail (or trough)
c) grasp wide of the shoulders
d) keep the arms straight

or

a) grasp over the rail (or trough)
b) grasp over the shoulders
c) keep the arms bent

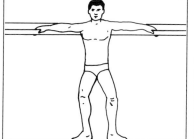
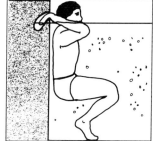

Raise the body

a) pull with the arms
b) kick the legs upwards

HORIZONTAL & EXTENDED POSITION

c) stretch the toes
d) point the toes
e) keep the chin in

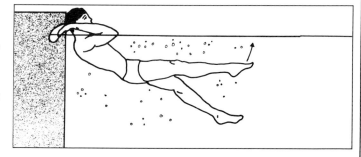

Lower the body
a) pull the legs to the wall
b) tuck the legs
c) bring the trunk towards the
   wall

Stand
a) bring the legs under the
   body
b) stretch the legs downwards
c) release the arms

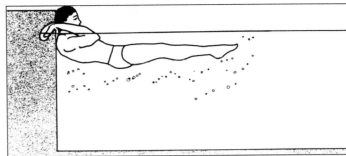

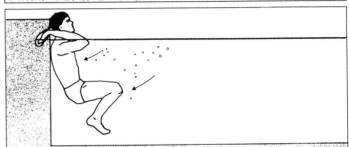

PRACTICE　3.　Hold the side of the pool: raise the body and legs to a side horizontal extended position and lower to place the feet on the bottom of the pcol.

TEACHING POINTS
Hold
a) face the pool side

TOP HAND
b) grasp over the rail (or trough)
c) keep the elbow against the
   wall

BOTTOM HAND
d) place the hand flat against
   the wall
e) place the hand underneath
   the top hand
f) point the fingers
   downwards
g) bend the arm

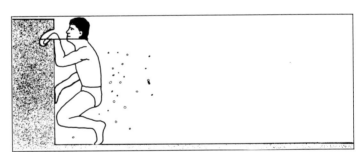

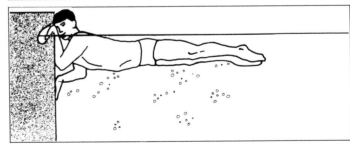

Raise the body
a) push with the bottom hand
b) pull with the top hand
c) pull and turn towards the
   bottom arm

SIDE HORIZONTAL & EXTENDED
POSITION
d) stretch the legs

e) point the toes
f) keep the chin in

Lower the body
a) pull the legs to the wall

b) pull and turn the body
c) turn the chest downwards
d) tuck the legs
e) lift the head
f) lift the trunk

PRACTICE 4. Stand one to two metres away facing the pool side: push and prone glide to the side and stand up. The distance from the pool side can be increased as the pupil becomes more competent.

TEACHING POINTS

Stand

a) keep the shoulders under the water
b) place the chin on the water
c) place the legs astride
d) bend the legs
e) point the fingers towards the wall
f) keep the palms downwards
g) stretch the arms
h) keep the arms under the water
i) bring the hands together

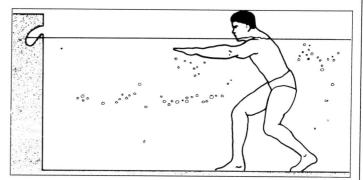

Push

a) drive the body forwards
b) push with the back leg
c) lift the legs
d) keep the shoulders under the water

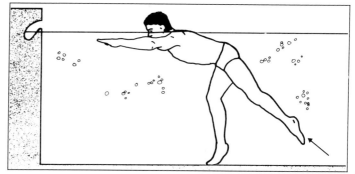

Glide

a) stretch the arms
b) reach for the wall
c) look downwards and forwards
d) place the head between the arms
e) squash the ears
f) stretch the legs

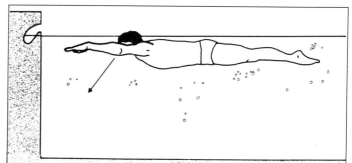

Contact with the side

a) push downwards on the rail (or trough)
b) lift the head
c) tuck the legs

Stand

a) bring the legs under the body
b) stretch the legs downwards
c) press the feet downwards

PRACTICE 5. Stand, holding a float, one to two metres away from and facing the pool side: push and prone glide to the side and stand up. The distance from the pool side can be increased as the pupil becomes more competent.

TEACHING POINTS

Stand
a) keep the shoulders under the water
b) place the chin on the water
c) place the legs astride
d) bend the legs

HOLD THE FLOAT
e) hold the sides of the float
f) hold half-way along
g) place the thumbs on top
h) keep the fingers underneath
i) straighten the arms

Push
a) drive the body forwards
b) push with the back leg
c) push forwards
d) lift the legs
e) keep the shoulders under the water

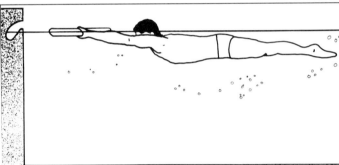

Glide
a) lock the arms
b) look forwards
c) keep the chin on the water
d) stretch the legs
e) reach with the float

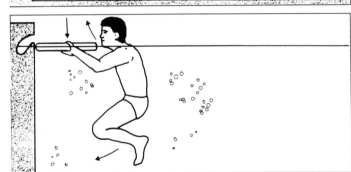

Contact with the side
a) press downwards on the float
b) lift the head
c) lift the trunk
d) tuck the legs

Stand
a) bring the legs under the body
b) stretch the legs downwards
c) press the feet downwards

PRACTICE 6. Stand facing the pool side: push backwards and away from the pool side and regain the standing position.

TEACHING POINTS

Stand
a) keep the shoulders under the water
b) place the chin on the water
c) face the pool side

Preparation
a) hold the rail (or trough) with both hands
b) hold shoulder-width apart
c) grasp over the rail (or trough)
d) place the feet against the wall
e) keep the feet low
f) look at the wall

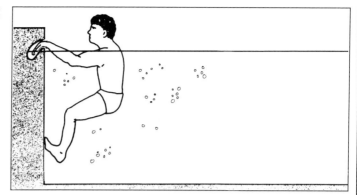

Sink
a) release and sink
b) sink and bend the arms
c) sink and bring the hands to the head
d) sink and salute
e) sink and bend the legs

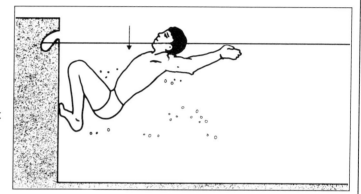

Push
a) push and stretch
b) keep the head between the arms
c) squash the ears
d) bring the hands together
e) keep the chin in

Glide
a) stretch from the fingertips to the toes

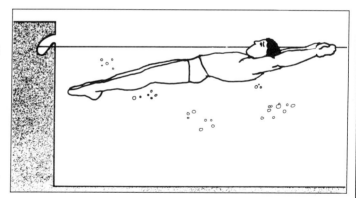

Glide ends
a) pull to the feet
b) bring the head forwards
c) tuck the legs

Stand
a) bring the legs under the body
b) stretch the legs downwards
c) press the feet downwards

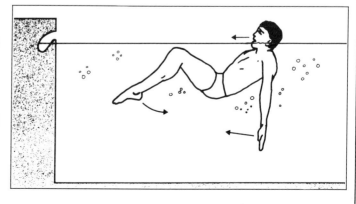

PRACTICE 7. Stand facing the pool side and holding a float: push backwards and away from the pool side and regain the standing position.

TEACHING POINTS

Stand
a) keep the shoulders under the water
b) place the chin on the water
c) place the legs astride
d) bend the legs

HOLD THE FLOAT
e) hold the sides of the float
f) hold half-way along
g) place the thumbs on top
h) keep the fingers underneath
i) rest the float on the surface
j) keep the arms straight
k) hold the float in front of the body

Push
a) drive the body backwards
b) push with the legs
c) push backwards
d) keep the shoulders under the water

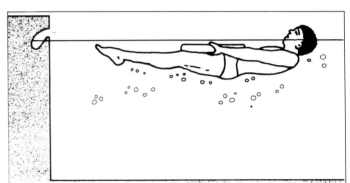

Glide
a) look upwards
b) rest the float on the surface
c) keep the legs close to the float
d) keep the arms straight
e) stretch the legs

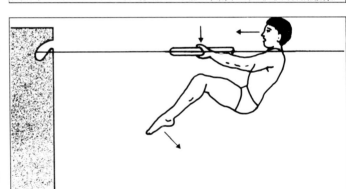

Glide ends
a) press downwards on the float
b) bring the head forwards
c) lift the trunk
d) tuck the legs

Stand
a) bring the legs under the body
b) stretch the legs downwards
c) press the feet downwards

PRACTICE 8. Stand with the back against the pool side: push and prone glide away from the pool side and regain the standing position.

TEACHING POINTS

Stand

a) keep the shoulders under the water
b) place the chin on the water
c) place the back against the pool side

Preparation

a) hold the rail (or trough) with both hands
b) hold wide of the shoulders
c) grasp over the rail (or trough)
d) place the feet against the wall
e) keep the feet low
f) look forwards
g) keep the shoulders under the water
h) place the chin on the water

Sink

a) release and sink
b) sink and bring the hands to the chin
c) sink and salute
d) sink and bend the legs

Push

a) push and stretch
b) keep the head between the arms
c) squash the ears
d) bring the hands together
e) look downwards and forwards
f) stretch from the fingertips to the toes

Regain the standing position

a) press the hands downwards
b) lift the head
c) tuck the legs
d) bring the legs under the body
e) stretch the legs downwards
f) press the feet downwards

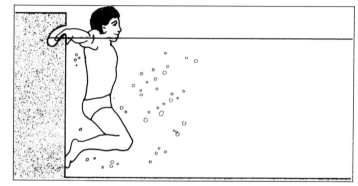

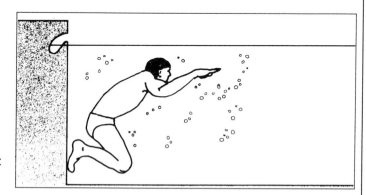

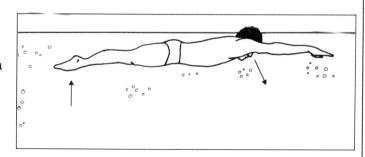

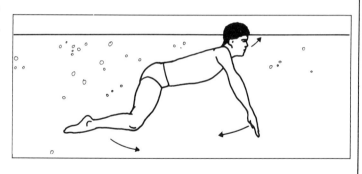

PRACTICE 9. Hold the side of the pool: raise the body and legs to an extended horizontal position and then a partner manually directs the leg movements. (Prone position).

TEACHING POINTS

Hold – subject

a) grasp over the rail (or trough)
b) bend the arms
c) keep the elbows against the wall

or

TOP HAND
a) grasp over the rail (or trough)
b) hold with stretched but slightly bent arm

BOTTOM HAND
c) place the hand against the wall
d) place the hand underneath
e) point the fingers downwards

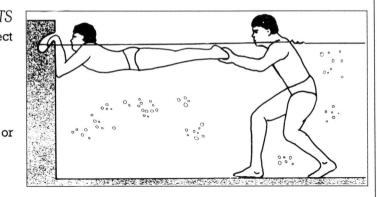

Hold – partner

a) hold the feet with each hand
b) separate the fingers from the thumbs
c) place the thumbs on the top
d) place the fingers underneath
e) guide the leg movements
f) keep the feet under the water

PRACTICE 10. Held by a partner: subject is towed in a prone position across the pool and helped to regain the feet.

TEACHING POINTS

Hold – subject

a) face the partner
b) overgrasp the arms
c) hold the upper arms
d) keep the arms straight

Hold – partner

a) face the subject
b) undergrasp the arms
c) hold underneath the elbows
d) keep the shoulders under the water

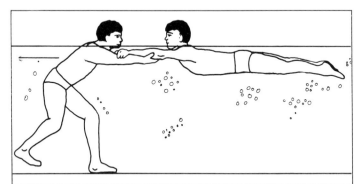

Pull – subject

a) keep the chin on the water
b) stretch the legs
c) stretch from the fingertips to the toes

Pull – partner

a) keep the subject's arms straight
b) keep the subject's arms in the water
c) slide the feet along the bottom of the pool
d) keep the chin on the water

Tow ends – subject

a) move the legs towards the partner
b) tuck the legs
c) lift the head

d) lift the trunk

Tow ends – partner
a) stand up
b) lift the subject's arms

Stand – subject
a) bring the legs under the
   body
b) stretch the legs downwards
c) press the feet downwards

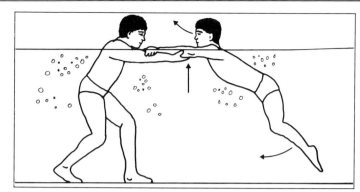

PRACTICE 11. Held by a partner: subject is towed in a supine position across the pool and helped to regain the feet.

TEACHING POINTS

Hold – partner
a) stand behind the subject
b) grasp under the armpits
c) keep the arms straight
d) keep the shoulders under
   the water
e) keep the chin on the water

Pull – subject
a) look upwards
b) stretch the legs
c) push the hips upwards
d) keep the arms at the side

Pull – partner
a) keep the arms straight
b) slide the feet along the
   bottom of the pool
c) keep the chin on the water

Tow ends – subject
a) push the hands towards
   the feet
b) tuck the legs
c) bring the head forwards
d) lift the trunk
e) stand up

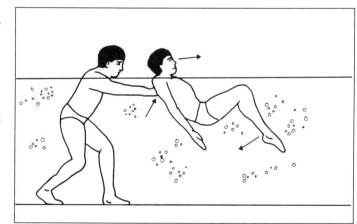

Tow ends - partner
a) lift the subject's trunk
b) push the subject's trunk
   forwards

Stand – subject
a) bring the legs under the
   body

b) stretch the legs
   downwards
c) press the feet downwards

Early water practices   1. Hold the side of the pool: the subject practises the leg movements (prone, supine or side position).

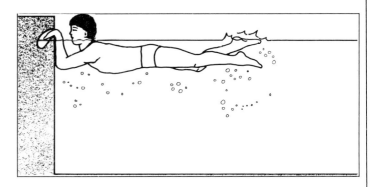

2. Partner grasps the subject: the subject practises the leg movements while being towed by the partner (prone or supine position).

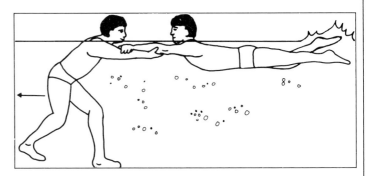

3. Stand one to two metres away from the pool side: the subject glides and then kicks several times before reaching the pool side (prone or side position).

4. Stand three to four metres away from the pool side and hold a float with arms extended beyond the head: the subject glides and then kicks to the pool side (prone or side position).

5. Stand with the feet astride (fore and aft) and the trunk resting horizontally along the water surface: the subject practises the arm movements and, later, the breathing rhythm (prone or side).

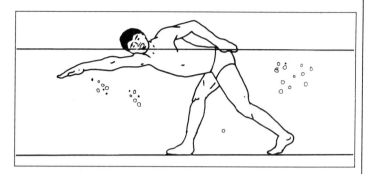

6. Stand with the feet astride (fore and aft) and the trunk resting horizontally along the water surface: the subject walks and practises the arm movement and, later, the breathing rhythm (prone or side).

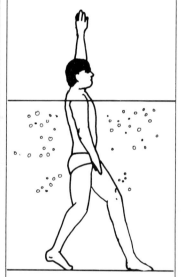

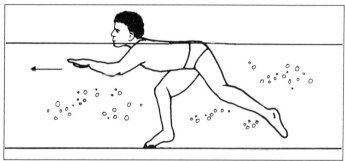

7. Stand with the feet astride (fore and aft) and the shoulders beneath the water surface: the subject practises the arm movements of the backstrokes.

8. Hold the pool side with the arm opposite to the

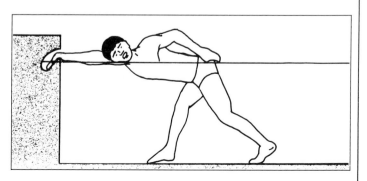

breathing side, keep the arm extended, the feet astride (fore and aft) and the trunk resting horizontally along the water surface: the subject practises the arm movements of the free arm and the breathing rhythm (frontcrawl and sidestroke).

9. Stand one to two metres away from the pool side: the subject glides and then pulls and kicks several times before reaching the pool side (prone or side position).

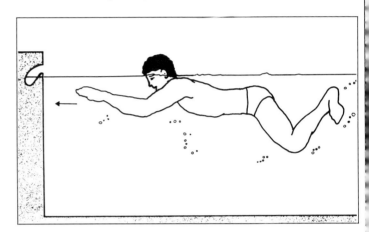

10. Stand at the pool side and hold a float with arms extended beyond the head: the subject pushes away from the pool side, glides and then kicks for several metres (prone or side position). For the supine position it is better to hold the float above the hips.

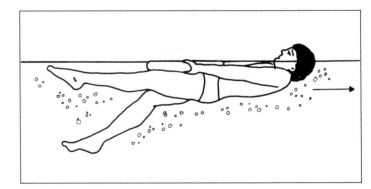

11. Stand at the pool side and hold a float with arms extended beyond the head: the subject pushes away from the pool side, glides and then kicks until the legs drop (prone or side position). For the supine position it is better to hold the float above the hips.

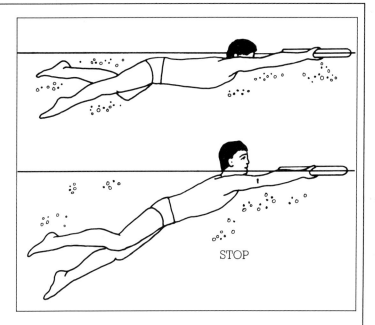

STOP

12. Stand at the pool side: the subject pushes away from the pool side, kicks and sculls with the hands close to the hips for several metres (supine position).

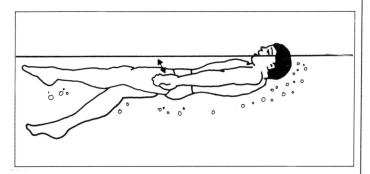

13. Stand at the pool side: the subject pushes away from the pool side, glides and then pulls and kicks for several metres (prone, supine or side position).

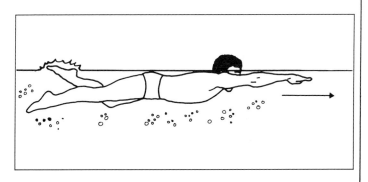

14. Stand at the pool side: the subject pushes away from the pool side, glides and then pulls and kicks until the legs drop (prone, supine or side position).

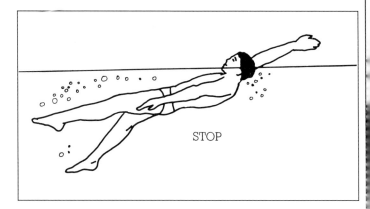

15. Subject is fitted with an artificial aid (e.g. rubber ring, arm bands): the subject practises leg, arm or combined movements (prone, supine or side position).

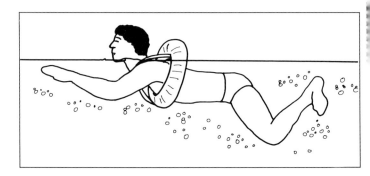

16. Stand in chest-depth water away from the pool side: the subject takes a deep breath, places the face in the water, rounds the back and holds below the knees (mushroom float). The majority of children will find that they are floaters as their backs will break the water surface.

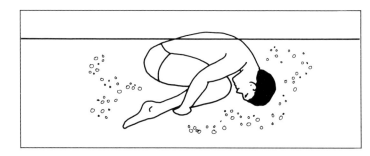

Later water practices   1. Stand one to two metres away from the pool side and hold a float between the upper legs: the subject glides to the pool side (prone or side position).

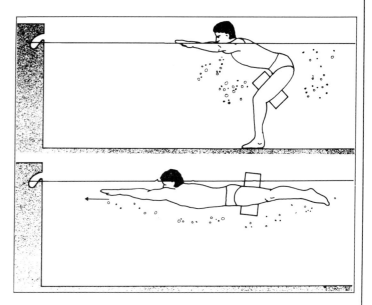

2. Stand three to four metres away from the pool side and hold a float between the upper legs: the subject glides and then pulls to the pool side (prone, or side position).

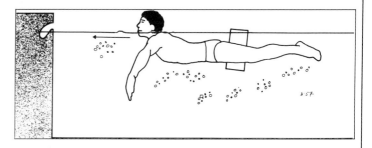

3. Stand at the pool side and hold a float between the upper legs: the subject glides away from the pool side (prone, supine or side position).

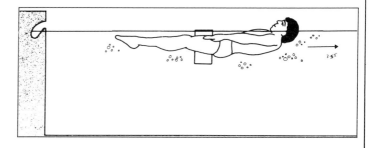

4. Stand at the pool side and hold a float between the upper legs: the subject glides and pulls for several metres (prone, supine or side position).

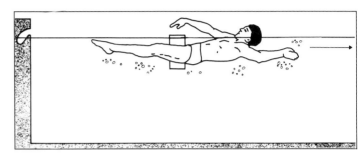

5. Stand at the pool side and hold a float between the upper legs: the subject glides and pulls for at least five metres (prone, supine or side position).

More advanced water practices

1. Stand at the pool side and hold a float with arms extended: the subject pushes away from the pool side and practises the leg movements for ten metres or more (prone, supine or side position).

2. Stand at the pool side and hold a float at right angles with arms extended: the subject pushes away from the pool side and practises the leg movements for ten metres or more (prone, supine or side position).

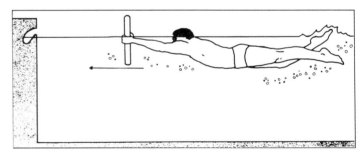

3. Stand at the pool side with the arms extended beyond the head: the subject pushes away from the pool side and

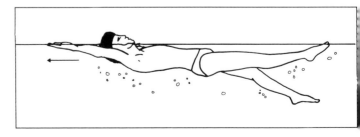

practises the leg movements for ten metres or more (prone, supine or side position).

4. Stand at the pool side with arms clasped behind the back: the subject pushes away from the pool side and practises the leg movements for ten metres or more (prone, supine or side position).

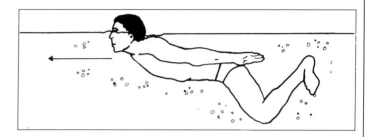

5. Hold the side of the pool with bent arms: the subject vigorously pushes away from the pool side (i.e. feet first) and then kicks to return to the side (prone or side position).

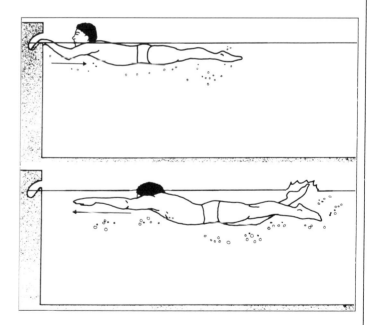

6. Hold a float between the upper legs: the subject pushes away from the pool side and practises the arm actions for several widths (prone, supine or side position).

7. The subject pushes away from the pool side and practises the arm actions while trailing the legs.

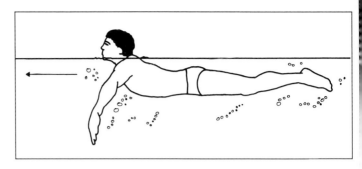

8. Extend one arm beyond the head and hold a float: the subject pushes away from the pool side and practises the leg movements and the arm actions of the free arm (prone, supine or side position).

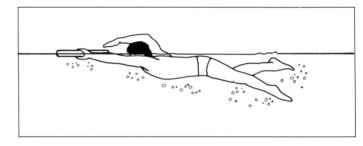

9. Extend one arm beyond the head: the subject pushes away from the pool side and practises the leg movements and the arm actions of the free arm (prone, supine or side position).

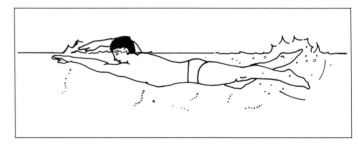

Further stroke drills At a competitive level coaches use many different types of aids and additional practices that are of a general nature or specific to a stroke. Pull-buoys, wrist weights, fins, hand paddles and drag suits are examples of aids that are used regularly in a club environment. Closing the hands while doing arm drills and practising the breaststroke leg kick with the knees close together are examples of general and specific stroke practices respectively.

4 ELEMENTARY DIVING

Early diving practices in shallow water

1. Stand in chest-depth water and hold the pool side with both hands: the subject submerges the head and quickly re-surfaces.

2. Stand in chest-depth water and hold the pool side with both hands: the subject submerges and re-surfaces the head several times, inhaling each time on re-surfacing.

3. Stand in chest-depth water and hold the pool side with both hands: the subject submerges the head with the eyes open, looks around underwater for several seconds and re-surfaces.

4. Stand in chest-depth water and hold the pool side with both hands: the subject submerges the head, blows out under water and re-surfaces.

5. Stand in chest-depth water and hold the pool side with one or both hands: the subject, with eyes open, sub-

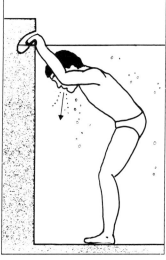

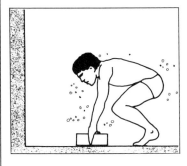

merges and re-surfaces the head several times, inhaling each time on re-surfacing and blowing out under the water.

6. Stand in chest-depth water close to the pool side: the subject, with eyes open, submerges by crouching down and picks up an object.

7. Stand, slightly crouched, in chest-depth water with the back to the pool side and the arms extended along the water surface: the subject places one foot against the wall, inhales, puts the face in the water and brings the other leg to the wall. With both feet against the wall and the trunk, head and arms in a horizontal plane and in line, the subject extends the legs and glides along the water surface. From this practice onwards the subject must ensure that the arms enclose and remain above the head, the hands are kept together with the palms facing downwards and the eyes are open.

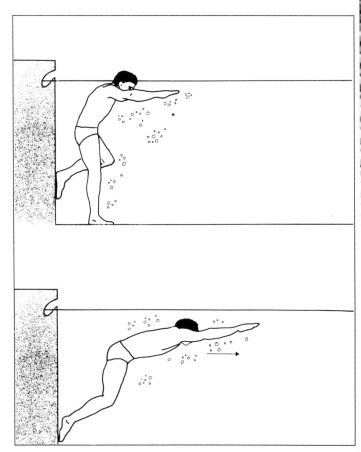

8. Stand, slightly crouched, in chest-depth water with the back to the pool side and the arms extended and pointing slightly downwards: the subject places one foot against the wall, inhales, puts the face in the water and brings the other leg to the wall. With both feet against the wall and the trunk, head and arms in line and directed forwards and downwards, the subject extends the legs and glides to the bottom of the pool. On touching the pool bottom the subject pushes the head and trunk upwards, tucks the legs beneath the body and stands up.

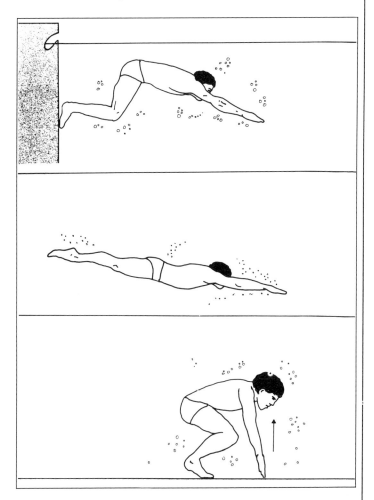

9. Stand, slightly crouched, in chest-depth water with the back to the pool side and the arms extended and pointing slightly downwards: the subject places one foot against the wall, inhales, puts the face in the water and brings the other leg to the wall. With both feet against the wall the trunk, head and arms in line and directed forwards and

downwards, the subject extends the legs and glides towards the bottom of the pool. When close to the bottom of the pool, the subject directs the fingers to the water surface, arches the back very gently and re-surfaces. Sometimes the subject might push and glide through a partner's legs before re-surfacing or, on touching the pool bottom, tuck and bring the hips over the arms and extend into an armstand first.

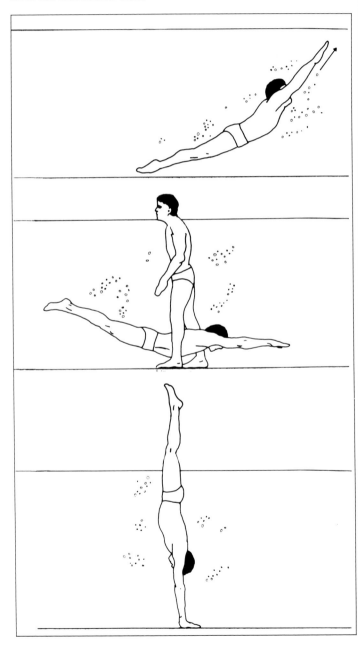

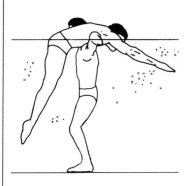

10. Stand, slightly crouched, in chest-depth water and face away from the pool side. Bring the hands of the extended arms together above the head and press the arms against the ears. Point the fingers upwards and face the palms forwards. A partner places an extended arm horizontally along the water surface and in front of the subject's chest. The subject then bends the legs and pikes slightly at the hips, drives the hips upwards, dives in a pike position over the extended arm and enters the water head first. The arms remain above the head until the subject has glided back to the water surface by gently arching and directing the fingers upwards.

Early diving practices from the pool side

Although the depth of water for pool side entries could vary according to the size of the subjects and the type of movement, it is far safer to practise in deep water (three to three-and-a-half metres).

1. JUMP

Jump feet first into the water from the pool side.

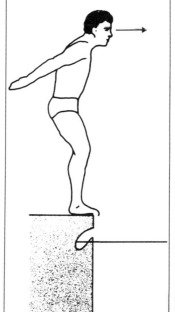
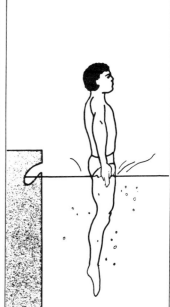

TEACHING POINTS

Basic position
a) grip the toes over the pool side
b) place the arms at the sides of the body

Take-off
a) bend the legs and drive outwards
b) drive outwards and upwards
c) swing the arms backwards and forwards
d) drive and swing
e) look forwards

Flight
a) stretch the arms down the side of the body

or

a) stretch the arms above the head
b) stretch the body and limbs
c) tense

Entry
a) stretch the body and limbs

b) stretch the toes
c) hold the legs together

either

d) hold the arms close to the body

e) keep the arms straight

f) place the palms against the body **or**

d) stretch the arms above the head

e) squeeze the ears between the arms

f) keep the arms straight

g) face the palms forwards

h) hold the thumbs together

Submersion

a) sink and stretch

b) kick and pull to the water surface

2. SITTING DIVE Sit on the pool side with the heels resting on the rail or trough. Round the back, enclose the ears between the extended arms, hold the hands together, keep the palms downwards and point the fingers at the water surface approximately one metre from the pool side. The subject overbalances and, keeping the head between the arms, stretches for the water. The subject keeps the feet in contact with the pool side for as long as possible. A late push to lift the hips upwards and achieve a slightly steeper entry can be encouraged once the subject copes successfully with the simple overbalance. After complete submersion and a short glide the subject directs the fingers upwards, gently arches the body and kicks to the water surface. The arms are used once the subject has directed the body upwards. If the bottom of the pool was touched with the hands, the subject pushes upwards, tucks the body and kicks and pulls to the water surface.

TEACHING POINTS

Basic position

a) sit on the edge of the pool

b) rest the heels on the trough (or rail)

c) keep the heels together

d) keep the knees together

e) round the back

f) straighten the arms

g) point the fingers at the water surface

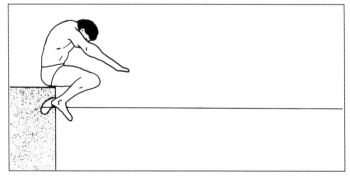

h) point at a mark one metre
away
i) hold the thumbs together
j) face the palms downwards
k) keep the head down
between the arms
l) squeeze the ears between
the arms

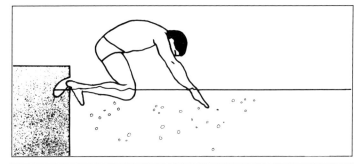

Overbalance

a) overbalance and stretch
the arms
b) keep the head between the
arms
c) keep the heels on the
trough (or rail)

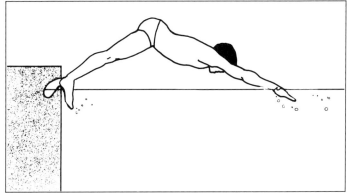

Entry

a) stretch the arms
b) stretch the fingers
c) keep the head between the
arms
d) keep the feet on the trough
(or rail)
e) enter and lift the hips (later
stage)
f) enter and straighten the
legs (later stage)

Submersion

a) sink and stretch
b) sink and glide
c) stretch the body and limbs
d) stretch from the fingertips
to the toes

e) keep the eyes open

Bottom of the pool reached
a) push upwards with the
hands
b) tuck the legs
c) drive off the botttom
d) look to the surface
e) look upwards
f) kick and pull to the surface

**or Bottom of the pool
not reached**
a) direct the fingers upwards
b) look to the surface
c) look upwards
d) arch the body gently
e) keep the head between
the arms
f) kick to the surface
g) kick to the surface and pull

3. KNEELING DIVE

Kneel on the pool side with the knee of one leg in line
with the edge and the toes of the other leg gripping round
the edge of the pool. Round the back, enclose the ears
between the extended arms, hold the hands together,
keep the palms downwards and point the fingers at the
water surface approximately one metre from the pool
side. The subject overbalances and, keeping the head
between the arms, stretches for the water. The subject
keeps the knee and the foot in contact with the pool side
for as long as possible. A late extension of the legs to lift
the hips upwards and achieve a slightly steeper entry can

be encouraged once the subject performs the kneeling dive by simply overbalancing. After complete submersion and a short glide the subject directs the fingers upwards, gently arches the body and kicks to the water surface.

TEACHING POINTS

Basic position

a) kneel on the edge of the pool
b) place one knee on the edge of the pool
c) grip the toes of one foot round the edge
d) keep the knee and front foot close together
e) round the back
f) straighten the arms
g) point the fingers at the water surface
h) point at a mark one metre away
i) hold the thumbs together
j) face the palms downwards
k) keep the head down between the arms
l) squeeze the ears

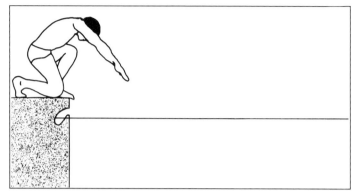

Overbalance

a) overbalance and stretch the arms
b) keep the head between the arms
c) keep the knee on the pool side
d) keep the foot on the pool side

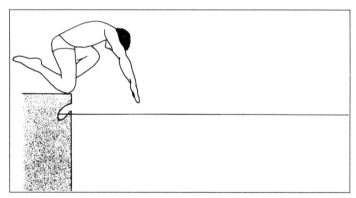

Entry

a) stretch the arms
b) stretch the fingers
c) keep the head between the arms
d) keep the knee and foot on the pool side
e) enter and lift the hips (later stage)
f) enter and straighten the legs (later stage)

Submersion

a) sink and stretch
b) sink and glide
c) stretch the body and limbs
d) stretch from the fingertips to the toes
e) keep the eyes open

Bottom of the pool reached

a) push upwards with the hands
b) tuck the legs
c) drive off the bottom
d) look to the surface

e) look upwards
f) kick and pull to the surface

or Bottom of the pool not reached

a) direct the fingers upwards
b) look to the surface
c) look upwards
d) arch the body gently
e) keep the head between the arms
f) kick to the surface
g) kick to the surface and pull

4. LOW CROUCH DIVE Stand in a low crouch position on the pool side with the legs slightly apart and the toes of both feet gripping round the edge of the pool. Round the back, enclose the ears between the extended arms, hold the hands together, keep the palms downwards and point the fingers at the water surface approximately one metre away from the pool side. The subject overbalances and, keeping the head between the arms, stretches for the water. The subject keeps the feet in contact with the pool side as long as possible. A late push to lift the hips higher and to achieve a slightly steeper entry can be encouraged once the subject performs the crouch dive by simply over-balancing. After complete submersion and a short glide the subject directs the fingers upwards, gently arches the body and kicks to the water surface. The arms are used once the subject has directed the body upwards. If the bottom of the pool is touched with the hands, the subject pushes upwards, tucks the body and kicks and pulls to the water surface.

TEACHING POINTS

Basic position

a) crouch on the edge of the pool
b) bend deeply at the hips and knees
c) place the feet hip-width apart
d) grip the toes round the edge of the pool
e) lower the body
f) round the back
g) straighten the arms
h) point the fingertips at the water surface
i) point at a mark one metre away
j) hold the thumbs together
k) face the palms downwards
l) keep the head down between the arms
m) squeeze the ears

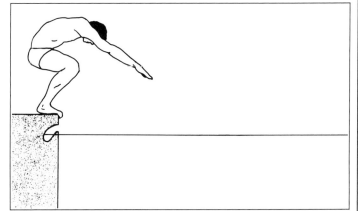

Overbalance

a) overbalance and stretch the arms

b) keep the head between the arms
c) keep the feet on the pool side

Entry
a) stretch the arms
b) stretch the fingers
c) keep the head between the arms
d) keep the feet on the pool side
e) enter and lift the hips (later stage)
f) enter and straighten the legs (later stage)

g) enter and push upwards (later stage)
h) push with the toes

Submersion
a) sink and stretch
b) sink and glide
c) stretch the body and limbs
d) stretch from the fingertips to the toes
e) keep the eyes open

Bottom of the pool reached
a) push upwards with the hands

b) tuck the legs
c) drive off the bottom
d) look to the surface
e) look upwards
f) kick and pull to the surface

or Bottom of the pool not reached
a) direct the fingers upwards
b) look to the surface
c) look upwards
d) arch the body gently
e) keep the head between the arms
f) kick to the surface
g) kick to the surface and pull

5. LUNGE DIVE

Stand, slightly crouched, on the pool side with the toes of one foot gripping round the edge of the pool and the other foot about a half-a-metre back and a little to one side. Round the back, enclose the ears between the extended arms, hold the hands together, keep the palms downwards and point the fingers at the water surface approximately one metre away from the pool side. The subject overbalances, lifts the back leg and stretches for entry. The head is kept between the arms and the front foot is kept in contact with the pool side for as long as possible. As the entry is made the front leg is brought in line with the body and the other leg. After complete submersion and a short glide the subject directs the fingers upwards, gently arches the body and kicks to the water surface. The arms are used once the subject has directed the body upwards. If the bottom of the pool is touched with the hands, the subject pushes upwards, tucks the body and kicks and pulls to the water surface.

TEACHING POINTS
Basic position
a) place one foot on the edge of the pool
b) place the other foot a half-metre behind and to one side
c) bend at the hips and knees
d) lower the body
e) round the back
f) straighten the arms

g) point the fingertips at the water surface
h) point at a mark one metre away
i) hold the thumbs together
j) face the palms downwards
k) keep the head down between the arms
l) squeeze the ears

Overbalance
a) overbalance slowly
b) lift the back leg
c) stretch the back leg
d) stretch the arms
e) keep the head between the arms
f) keep the front foot on the pool side

Entry
a) stretch the arms
b) stretch the fingers
c) keep the head between the arms
d) enter and push with the front foot
e) push and lift the front leg
f) bring the front leg in line with the body

Submersion
a) sink and stretch
b) sink and glide
c) stretch the body and limbs
d) stretch from the fingertips to the toes
e) keep the eyes open

Bottom of the pool reached
a) push upwards with the hands
b) tuck the legs
c) drive off the bottom

d) look to the surface
e) look upwards
f) kick and pull to the surface

or Bottom of the pool not reached
a) direct the fingers upwards
b) look to the surface
c) look upwards
d) arch the body gently
e) keep the head between the arms
f) kick to the surface
g) kick to the surface and pull

6 SEMI-CROUCH DIVE

Stand in a semi-crouch position on the pool side with the legs slightly apart and the toes of both feet gripping round the edge of the pool. Round the back, enclose the ears between the extended arms, hold the hands together, keep the palms downwards and point the fingers at the water surface approximately two metres away from the pool side. The subject overbalances and, keeping the head between the arms, vigorously extends the legs and stretches for the water. After complete submersion and a short glide the subject directs the fingers upwards, gently arches the body and kicks to the water surface. The arms are used once the subject has directed the body upwards. If the bottom of the pool is touched with the hands, the subject pushes upwards, tucks the body and kicks and pulls to the water surface.

TEACHING POINTS

Basic position

a) crouch on the edge of the pool
b) bend at the hips and knees
c) place the feet hip-width apart
d) grip the toes round the edge of the pool
e) lower the body
f) round the back
g) straighten the arms
h) point the fingertips at the water surface
i) point at a mark two metres away
j) hold the thumbs together
k) face the palms downwards
l) keep the head down between the arms
m) squeeze the ears

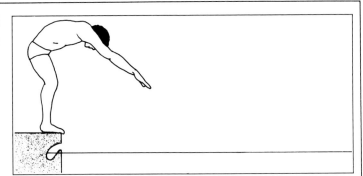

Overbalance

a) overbalance and stretch the arms
b) keep the head between the arms
c) overbalance and drive with the legs
d) drive the hips upwards
e) straighten the legs vigorously
f) push with the toes

Flight

a) stretch from the fingertips to the toes
b) squeeze the ears
c) stretch in flight

Entry

a) stretch the arms
b) stretch the fingers
c) stretch from the fingertips to the toes

Submersion

a) sink and stretch
b) sink and glide
c) stretch the body and limbs

d) stretch from the fingertips to the toes
e) keep the eyes open

Bottom of the pool reached

a) push upwards with the hands
b) tuck the legs
c) drive off the bottom
d) look to the surface
e) look upwards

f) kick and pull to the surface

or Bottom of the pool not reached

a) direct the fingers upwards
b) look to the surface
c) look upwards
d) arch the body gently
e) keep the head between the arms
f) kick to the surface
g) kick to the surface and pull

Progression to a plunge dive

SEMI-CROUCH DIVE WITH LONG GLIDE

Stand in a semi-crouch position on the pool side with the legs slightly apart and the toes of both feet gripping round the edge of the pool. Round the back, enclose the ears between the extended arms, hold the hands together, keep the palms downwards and point the fingers at the water surface approximately two metres away from the pool side. The subject overbalances, keeps the feet in contact with the pool side as long as possible and then, keeping the head between the arms, drives the body vigorously outwards. The subject keeps the body rigid, glides just under the water surface and directs the fingers to the water surface as the speed decreases.

TEACHING POINTS

Basic position

a) crouch on the edge of the pool
b) bend at the hips and knees
c) place the feet hip-width apart
d) grip the toes round the edge of the pool
e) lower the body
f) round the back
g) straighten the arms
h) point the fingertips at the water surface
i) point at a mark two metres away
j) hold the thumbs together
k) face the palms downwards
l) keep the head down between the arms
m) squeeze the ears

Overbalance

a) overbalance and stretch the arms
b) keep the head between the arms
c) overbalance and drive with the legs
d) drive the body outwards
e) keep foot contact
f) push vigorously with the toes

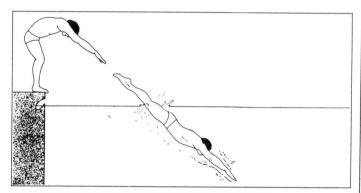

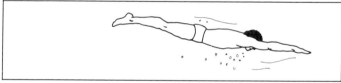

Flight

a) stretch from the fingertips to the toes
b) squeeze the ears
c) stretch in flight

Entry

a) stretch the arms
b) stretch the fingers
c) stretch from the fingertips to the toes

Submersion and glide

a) sink and stretch
b) sink and glide
c) stretch the body and limbs
d) stretch from the fingertips

to the toes
e) keep the eyes open
f) stretch towards the opposite wall
g) point the fingers towards the opposite wall
h) keep the head between the arms
i) squeeze the ears

Surface

a) direct the fingers upwards
b) arch the body gently
c) keep the head between the arms
d) bring the head up as the body slows

Plunge dive

Stand in a semi-crouch position on the pool side with the legs slightly apart and the toes of both feet gripping round the edge of the pool. Round the back, lift the arms upwards and backwards to just behind the hips so that the palms are facing backwards and upwards. Look forwards and downwards at a point just beyond entry. The subject overbalances, swings the arms forwards and upwards and pushes vigorously from the pool side. The ears are enclosed by the arms as the hands come together beyond the head. The subject stretches from the fingertips to the toes and enters the water in a streamlined position with the body firm, and the head between the arms. The subject keeps the body rigid, glides just under the surface and directs the fingers to the surface as the speed decreases.

TEACHING POINTS

Basic position

a) crouch on the edge of the pool
b) bend at the hips and knees
c) place the feet hip-width apart
d) grip the toes round the edge of the pool
e) lower the body
f) round the back
g) lift the arms
h) face the palms backwards
i) place the hands behind the hips
j) look forwards and downwards
k) look at a point two metres away

Overbalance

a) overbalance and swing the arms forwards
b) swing and stretch the arms forwards
c) drop the head between the arms
d) overbalance and drive with the legs
e) drive the body outwards
f) keep foot contact
g) push vigorously with the toes

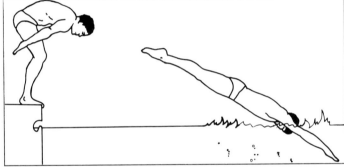

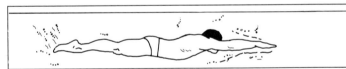

Flight

a) stretch from the fingertips to the toes
b) squeeze the ears
c) stretch in flight
d) keep the eyes open
e) stretch towards the opposite wall
f) point the fingers towards the opposite wall
g) keep the head between the arms
h) squeeze the ears

Entry

a) stretch the arms
b) stretch the fingers
c) stretch from the fingertips to the toes

Submersion and glide

a) sink and stretch
b) sink and glide
c) stretch from the fingertips to the toes

Surface

a) direct the fingers upwards
b) arch the body gently
c) keep the head between the arms
d) bring the head up as the body slows

Progressions to a plain header

1. HIGH-CROUCH DIVE

Stand in a semi-crouch position on the pool side with the legs together and the toes of both feet gripping round the edge of the pool. Extend the arms above the head, bring the hands together with the palms facing forwards and keep the head between the arms. Bend forwards slightly at the hips. The subject overbalances and immediately drives the hips vigorously upwards. A slight hip bend is maintained in flight and the body and limbs are kept firm. The legs are brought in line with the body and arms on entry and the subject stretches from the fingertips to the toes. After complete submersion the subject glides towards the bottom of the pool. If the bottom is not reached, the subject directs the fingers upwards, gently arches the back and kicks to the water surface. The arms are used once the subject has directed the body upwards. If the bottom of the pool is reached, the subject pushes upwards, tucks the body, kicks and pulls to the water surface.

TEACHING POINTS

Basic position

a) crouch on the edge of the pool
b) bend at the hips and knees
c) place the feet together
d) grip the toes round the edge of the pool
e) lower the body
f) straighten the arms
g) hold the thumbs together
h) face the palms downwards
i) keep the head down between the arms
j) squeeze the ears

Take-off

a) overbalance and drive the hips upwards
b) lose balance and drive immediately
c) drive upwards vigorously
d) keep the head between the arms
e) overbalance and stretch the arms

f) straighten the legs
vigorously
g) push with the toes

Flight

a) maintain a slight bend at
the hips
b) keep the body firm
c) stretch the arms
d) squeeze the ears
e) stretch the fingers
f) stretch the legs
g) stretch the toes

Entry

a) stretch the arms
b) stretch the fingers
c) straighten the legs at the
hips
d) stretch from the fingertips
to the toes

Submersion

a) sink and stretch
b) sink and glide
c) stretch the body
d) stretch from the fingertips
to the toes

e) keep the eyes open

Bottom of the pool reached

a) push upwards with the
hands
b) tuck the legs
c) drive off the bottom
d) look to the surface
e) look upwards
f) kick and pull to the surface

**or Bottom of the pool
not reached**

a) direct the fingers upwards
b) look to the surface
c) look upwards
d) arch the body gently
e) keep the head between
the arms
f) kick to the surface
g) kick to the surface and pull

2. SPRING HEADER Stand in an upright position on the pool side with legs together and the toes of both feet gripping round the edge of the pool. Extend the arms beyond the head and point them outwards and upwards. Stretch the fingers and face the palms forwards. Look straight ahead and keep the head in line with the arms and the body. The subject then brings the body slightly forwards. Once this position has been established the subject overbalances, bends at the knees and drives the hips upwards. The hands are brought together above the head during the flight, and the legs are brought in line with the body on entry. After complete submersion, the subject glides towards the bottom of the pool. If the bottom is not reached the subject directs the fingers upwards, gently arches the back and kicks to the water surface. The arms are used once the subject has directed the body upwards. If the bottom of the pool is reached the subject pushes upwards, tucks the body, kicks and pulls to the water surface.

TEACHING POINTS

Basic position

a) stand upright

b) place the feet together

c) grip the toes round the edge of the pool

d) stretch the arms above the head

e) point the arms diagonally upwards

f) face the palms forwards

g) stretch the fingers

h) look forwards

i) keep the head in line with the body

j) hold the body and limbs firm

Prepare for take-off

a) bring the body slightly forwards

Take-off

a) overbalance and bend the knees

b) bend at the knees and drive upwards

c) drive the hips upwards

d) lose balance and drive immediately

e) straighten the legs vigorously

f) push with the toes

g) stretch the arms

h) hold the 'Y' position

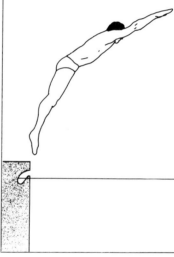

Flight

a) maintain a slight bend at the hips

b) keep the body firm

c) stretch the arms

d) bring the arms together

e) squeeze the ears

f) stretch the fingers

g) stretch the legs

h) stretch the toes

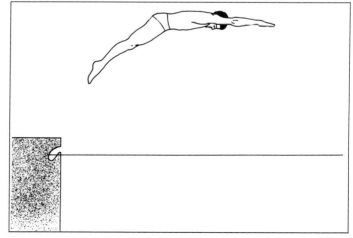

Entry
a) stretch the arms
b) stretch the fingers
c) straighten the legs at the hips
d) stretch from the fingertips to the toes

Submersion
a) sink and stretch
b) sink and glide
c) stretch the body
d) stretch from the fingertips to the toes
e) keep the eyes open

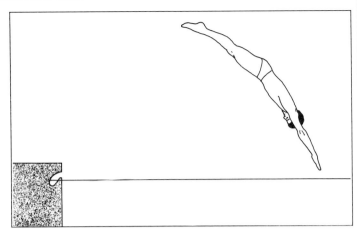

Bottom of the pool reached
a) push upwards with the hands
b) tuck the legs
c) drive off the bottom
d) look to the surface

e) look upwards
f) kick and pull to the surface

or Bottom of the pool not reached
a) direct the fingers upwards
b) look to the surface

c) look upwards
d) arch the body gently
e) keep the head between the arms
f) kick to the surface
g) kick to the surface and pull

Plain header

BASIC POSITION The diver stands in an upright position on the pool side with the legs together and the toes of both feet gripping round the edge of the pool. The arms are extended above the head and pointed outwards and upwards ('Y' position). The palms are facing forwards and the fingers and thumb of each hand are brought together. The diver looks forwards and holds the body and limbs firm.

TAKE-OFF The diver bends a little at the knees, brings the trunk slightly forwards, and quickly and vigorously drives the hips upwards as the body overbalances. With the final push from the feet, the diver stretches the legs and maintains the bent position at the hips, keeping the body, head and arms in line.

FLIGHT During most of the flight the diver keeps the body, head and limbs still. Just prior to entry the arms are brought together above the head and the legs are straightened at the hips. The diver's thumbs touch and the hands, with the palms facing backwards and slightly downwards, follow the line of the extended arms.

ENTRY The diver stretches from fingertips to toes and enters as close to the vertical as possible. The entry is through the fingertips and the arms, head, body and legs are held in a straight line. After complete submersion, the subject glides towards the bottom of the pool. If the bottom is not reached the subject directs the fingers upwards, gently arches the back and kicks to the water surface. The arms are used once the body is directed upwards. If the bottom of the pool is reached the subject pushes upwards, tucks the body, kicks and pulls to the water surface.

TEACHING POINTS

Basic position

a) stand upright
b) place the feet together
c) grip the toes round the edge of the pool
d) stretch the arms above the head
e) point the arms diagonally outwards
f) face the palms forwards
g) stretch the fingers
h) look forwards
i) keep the head in line with the body
j) hold the body and limbs firm

Prepare for take-off

a) bring the body slightly forwards

Take-off

a) overbalance and bend the knees
b) bend at the knees and drive upwards
c) drive the hips upwards
d) lose balance and drive immediately
e) straighten the legs vigorously
f) push with the toes
g) stretch the arms
h) hold the 'Y' position

Flight

a) maintain a slight bend at the hips

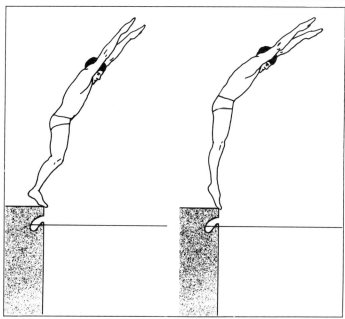

b) keep the limbs and body
   firm
c) keep the head still
d) keep the head in line with
   the body
e) stretch the legs
f) stretch the toes
g) look for the entry
h) spot the entry

JUST PRIOR TO ENTRY

i) close the arms
j) bring the arms together
k) squeeze the ears
l) hold the thumbs together

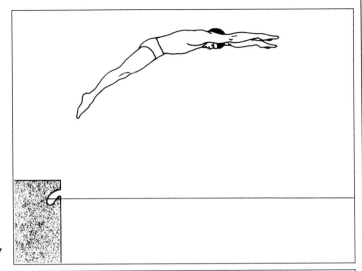

Entry

a) stretch the arms
b) stretch the fingers
c) straighten the legs at the
   hips
d) stretch from the fingertips
   to the toes

Submersion

a) sink and stretch
b) sink and glide
c) stretch the body and limbs
d) stretch from the fingertips
   to the toes
e) keep the eyes open

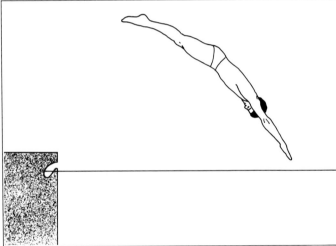

Bottom of the pool reached

a) push upwards with the
   hands
b) tuck the legs
c) drive off the bottom
d) look to the surface
e) look upwards
f) kick and pull to the surface

or Bottom of the pool not reached

a) direct the fingers upwards
b) look to the surface
c) look upwards
d) arch the body gently
e) keep the head between the
   arms
f) kick to the surface
g) kick to the surface and pull

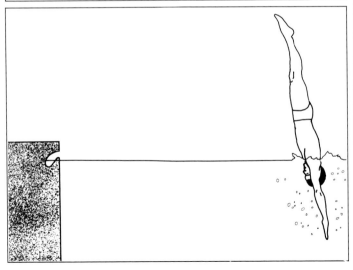

5 STARTS AND TURNS

Front start – conventional

TAKE YOUR MARKS The swimmer steps forwards and places the feet hip-width apart with the toes curled over the pool side or starting block. The trunk is bent forwards at the hips so that it is more or less at right angles to the legs. The back is rounded, the knees are partially flexed and the head is slightly raised. The arms are dropped downwards from the shoulders and held outside the line of the legs. The fingers point downwards and the palms face backwards. The swimmer looks forwards and downwards at a point just beyond the entry. The weight of the body is nicely balanced over the balls of the feet.

STARTING SIGNAL The swimmer falls forwards by dropping the head and shoulders and swinging the arms. In the circular backswing action the arms move upwards and outwards and then continue backwards, inwards and forwards in a circular fashion. In the straight backswing technique the swimmer swings the arms backwards and then forwards, and in the arms back movement the arms start behind the hips and then make a short swing upwards and backwards before swinging forwards. During the early part of the arm movement the swimmer continues to overbalance and drop so that the heels lift off the block. As the swimmer starts to swing the arms forwards a final inhalation before entry is taken and the leg drive commences. The angle at the knee joint before the drive outwards is approximately 90 degrees. The swimmer lifts the head and drives the body forwards vigorously. By stopping the hands short of the horizontal as the feet push off the block, the momentum gained during the swing helps in pulling the body outwards and slightly upwards.

FLIGHT The swimmer stretches from the fingertips to the toes and maintains a rigid position in flight. Just prior to the entry the arms are lifted slightly and the head is lowered between the arms.

ENTRY   The swimmer enters through the fingertips at a very narrow angle to the water surface. The breaststroker enters at a slightly steeper angle than the butterflyer and the frontcrawler enters nearest to the horizontal. The body is held firm and the limbs are stretched.

Front start – grab

NOTE: This is the start used by most competitive swimmers. The reasons for this are the stability of the starting position and the fact that it enables the swimmer to leave the block more quickly.

TAKE YOUR MARKS   The swimmer steps forwards and places the feet close together, but not touching, with the toes curled over the pool side or starting block. The front of the block is grasped outside the feet. Some swimmers place the feet about hip-width apart and grasp between the feet. The swimmer holds the head and trunk down, keeps the arms more or less straight, bends the knees and looks down-wards at the water. The heels are kept down and the weight is kept over the feet.

STARTING SIGNAL   The swimmer drops the head, and by vigorously bending the elbows, pulls the body downwards and forwards. As the overbalancing commences and the heels lift off the block, the swimmer starts to swing the arms forwards and inhales. As the leg drive is made, the head is raised, the body is straightened and the arms are brought forwards and upwards. The arms swing through to the horizontal position in preparation for a quick entry. With the final ankle extension the swimmer stretches, lowers the head and completes the inhalation.

FLIGHT   The swimmer drops the head between the arms and looks downwards at the water. The body and limbs are held in a firm and streamlined position.

ENTRY   The swimmer enters through the fingertips at a very narrow angle to the water surface. The breaststroker enters at a slightly steeper angle than the butterflyer and the frontcrawler enters nearest to the horizontal. The body is held firm and the limbs are stretched.

GENERAL NOTE: For a piked entry the head is lowered early on in the flight, the arms point downwards and the body bends.

After entry the hands are directed to the water surface during the glide phase. This is an advanced technique that needs good timing and, for safety reasons, must be practised in *deep* water.

GLIDE, PULL AND SURFACE – CONVENTIONAL AND GRAB STARTS

The swimmer performing the grab start does not drive out as far as the swimmer performing the conventional front start and, therefore, enters the water earlier and commences this phase sooner. Apart from this one difference the glide, pull and surfacing techniques are similar.

In all strokes the glide is made in a streamlined position with the head in line with the rest of the body. After a short glide to reach swimming speed, the frontcrawl and butterfly swimmers will commence the stroke. The frontcrawler kicks and pulls with one arm and raises the head slightly forwards. The swimmer's head breaks the water surface as the pulling arm is about to recover and the arm extended beyond the head is about to pull. The butterflyer kicks upwards, raises the head slightly and then starts to pull and to kick downwards. In both strokes the exhalation is made through the mouth and nose during this glide-pull phase and an inhalation may be taken either just after breaking the water surface or after a second arm pull has been made.

In breaststroke it takes longer to slow down to swimming speed than in frontcrawl or butterfly and, therefore, the glide is held for a longer time. The breaststroke swimmer either pulls outwards and backwards and then inwards with straight arms, or keeps the elbows high, moves the hands close together and finally extends the arms down the sides of the body. In both cases the hands finish close to the thighs and remain there for about one and a half seconds as a streamlined body position is maintained. The hands are then recovered near to the chest with the elbows kept close to the trunk. As the arms pass the chest, the legs start to recover. With the arms nearly straight the kick backwards is made and the head starts to rise to direct the body towards the surface. With the arms fully stretched and the legs almost together the head breaks the water surface. The second arm pull after the dive must not start until the head breaks the surface. During the latter part of the underwater sequence the swimmer exhales through the mouth and nose and is ready to inhale at the end of the second arm pull.

TEACHING POINTS – FRONT START (CONVENTIONAL)

Take your marks

a) curl the toes over the pool side

b) place the feet hip-width apart

c) bend forwards at the trunk

d) round the back

e) bend the knees

f) drop the arms downwards

g) point the fingers downwards

h) keep the palms facing backwards

i) hold the arms outside the legs

j) look forwards and downwards

k) look past the entry point

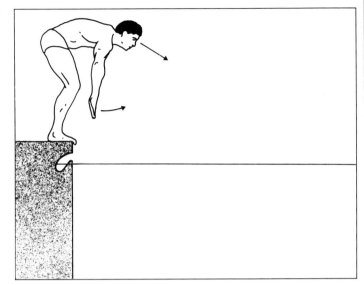

Starting signal: circular backswing

a) drop the head and shoulders

b) move the arms upwards and outwards

c) circle the arms backwards

d) wind up the arms

e) keep the arms straight

f) circle the arms and bend the knees

g) circle the arms and lower the trunk

h) circle the arms and drop

i) circle the arms and overbalance

j) swing the arms vigorously forwards

k) swing the arms forwards and raise the head

l) look forwards and downwards

m) swing the arms and straighten the legs

n) breathe in and move the arms forwards

o) reach with the arms

p) point the fingers downwards and forwards

q) stretch the arms and legs
r) stretch from the fingertips to the toes
s) push with the toes

or Starting signal: swing backwards and forwards (straight backswing)

a) swing the arms backwards
b) swing the arms and breathe in
c) swing the arms and overbalance
d) swing the arms and drop
e) swing the arms and bend the knees
f) keep the arms straight
g) drop the head and shoulders
h) swing the arms backwards and forwards
i) swing the arms vigorously forwards
j) swing the arms forwards and raise the head
k) look forwards and downwards
l) swing the arms and straighten the legs
m) reach with the arms
n) point the fingers downwards and forwards
o) stretch the arms and legs
p) stretch from the fingertips to the toes
q) push with the toes

or Starting signal: swing forwards (arms back)

a) hold the arms back
b) place the hands behind the hips
c) swing the arms upwards and backwards
d) swing the arms backwards and breathe in
e) swing the arms backwards and forwards

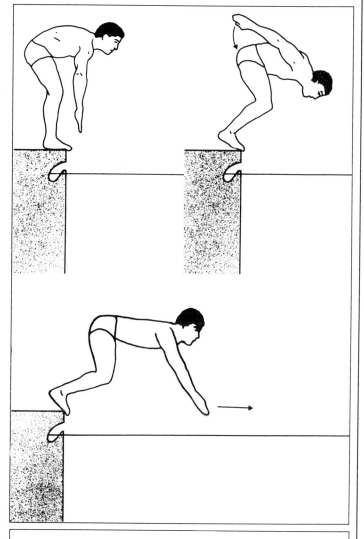

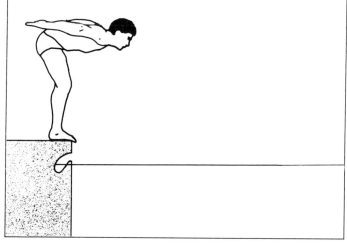

f) swing the arms forwards and drop
g) swing the arms forwards and bend the knees
h) keep the arms straight
i) drop the head and shoulders
j) look forwards and downwards
k) swing the arms and straighten the legs
l) reach with the arms
m) point the fingers downwards and forwards
n) stretch the arms and legs
o) stretch from the fingertips to the toes
p) push with the toes

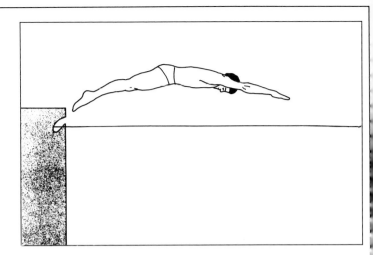

Flight

a) stretch in flight
b) stretch and lower the head
c) place the head between the arms
d) bring the arms together
e) stretch from the fingertips to the toes
f) reach for the entry
g) stretch for entry

Entry

a) enter through the fingertips
b) stretch on entry

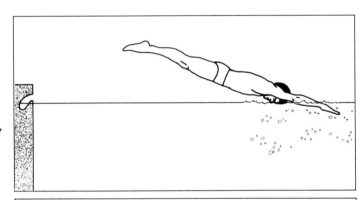

Glide, pull and surface: frontcrawl

a) sink and look forwards
b) glide briefly
c) point the fingers forwards and upwards
d) kick and pull together
e) glide, kick and pull with one arm
f) kick and pull to the surface
g) pull and raise the head
h) breathe out underwater
i) breathe out through the mouth and nose

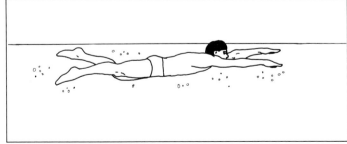

j) look to the side and breathe in
k) pull once and breathe in *or* pull twice and breathe in

or Glide, pull and surface: butterfly dolphin

a) sink and look forwards
b) stretch and glide

c) glide briefly
d) glide and bring the feet up
e) kick down and pull
f) kick and look forwards and upwards
g) glide, kick and pull to the surface
h) breathe out underwater
i) breathe out through the mouth and nose
j) pull and then breathe in *or* pull twice and then breathe in

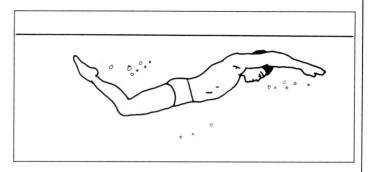

or Glide, pull and surface: breaststroke (a slightly steeper entry)

a) sink and keep the head down
b) stretch and glide
c) glide and then pull to the side
d) glide, pull, glide

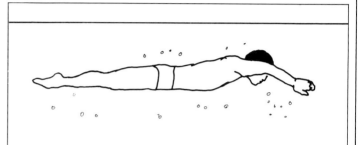

e) **either**
   i) pull outwards and to the side
   ii) keep the arms straight

   or
   i) pull out and backwards
   ii) bend and stretch the arms

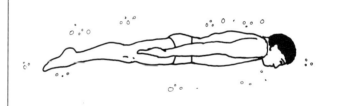

f) pull with the head down
g) pull, glide and recover
h) recover the arms and legs
i) recover the arms close to the body
j) bring the arms upwards close to the chest
k) stretch the arms and kick
l) kick and stretch to the surface
m) kick and lift the head
n) stretch the arms and lift the head
o) stretch to the surface
p) break the surface with the head

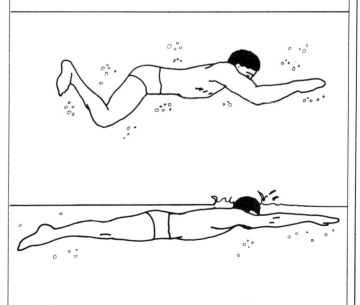

TEACHING POINTS – FRONT START (GRAB)

Starting position

a) curl the toes over the block

b)   **either**

   i) place the feet together

   ii) grasp outside the feet

           or

   i) place the feet apart

   ii) grasp between the feet

c) keep the heels down

d) grasp the front of the block

e) keep the trunk down

f) bend the knees

g) keep the head down

h) look down at the water

i) keep the arms straight

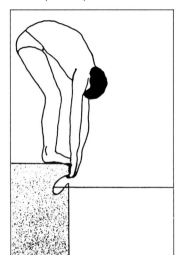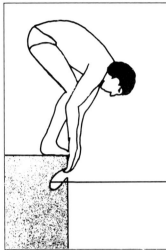

Starting signal

a) pull downwards and forwards

b) bend the elbows

c) keep the head down

d) pull and hold on

e) pull to overbalance

f) pull and raise the head

g) swing the arms forwards

h) overbalance and swing

i) overbalance and breathe in

j) straighten the legs

k) straighten the body

l) drive the body forwards

m) push with the toes

n) look forwards and downwards

o) stretch from the block

Flight

a) stretch and lower the head

b) stretch the arms forwards

c) lift the legs

d) hold the head between the arms

e) look downwards

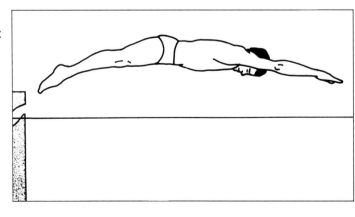

(OPPOSITE PAGE) *GRAB START (STARTING POSITION): keep the head down.*

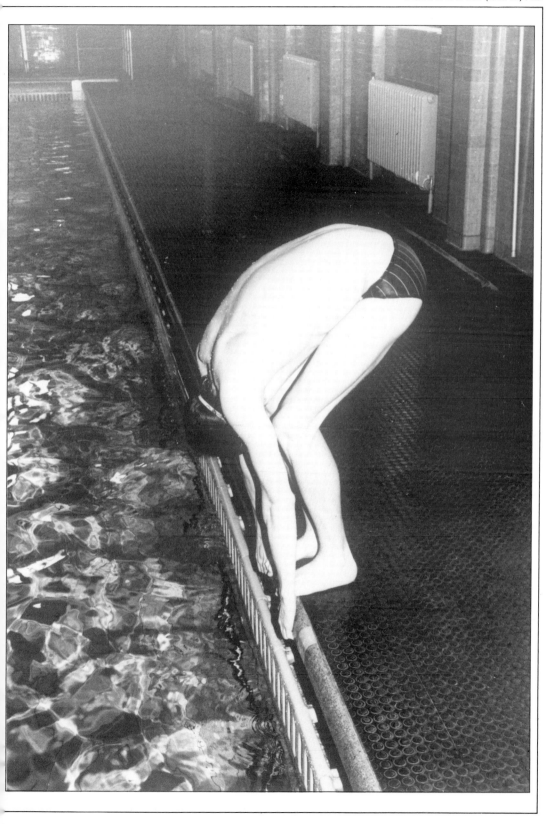

f) stretch from the fingertips
   to the toes
g) reach for the entry
h) stretch for entry

Entry

a) enter through the fingertips
b) stretch on entry

Piked entry

a) tuck the chin down in the
   early part of flight
b) bend at the waist
c) submerge, glide and direct
   the hands to the surface

Note: the piked flight and
entry is an advanced
technique and, for safety
reasons, must be practised in
deep water.

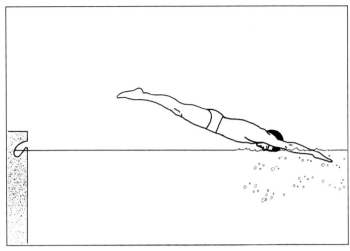

Glide, pull and surface: frontcrawl

a) sink and look forwards
b) glide briefly
c) point the fingers forwards
   and upwards
d) kick and pull together
e) glide, kick and pull with
   one arm
f) kick and pull to the surface
g) pull and raise the head
h) breathe out underwater
i) breathe out through the
   mouth and nose
j) look to the side and breathe
   in
k) pull once and breathe in *or*
   pull twice and breathe in

or Glide, pull and surface: butterfly dolphin

a) sink and look forwards
b) stretch and glide
c) glide briefly
d) glide and bring the feet up
e) kick down and pull
f) kick and look forwards and
   upwards

g) glide, kick and pull to the
   surface
h) breathe out underwater
i) breathe out through the
   mouth and nose
j) pull and then breathe in *or*
   pull twice and then breathe
   in

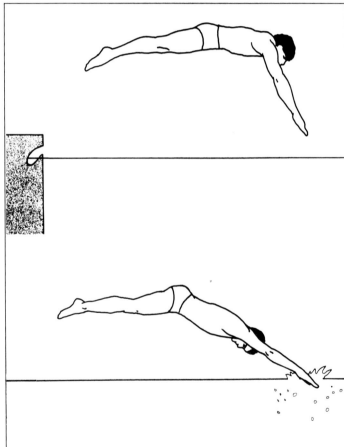

or Glide, pull and surface: breaststroke (a slightly steeper entry)

a) sink and keep the head down
b) stretch and glide
c) glide and then pull to the side
d) glide, pull, glide
e) **either**
    i) pull outwards and to the side
    ii) keep the arms straight **or**
    i) pull out and backwards
    ii) bend and stretch the arms
f) pull with the head down
g) pull, glide and recover
h) recover the arms and legs
i) recover the arms close to the body
j) bring the arms upwards close to the chest
k) stretch the arms and kick
l) kick and stretch to the surface
m) kick and lift the head
n) stretch the arms and lift the head
o) stretch to the surface
p) break the surface with the head

Backstroke start

STARTING POSITION   The swimmer overgrasps the block handholds, trough or rail. The arms are about shoulder-width apart and are straight. The feet can either be placed hip-width apart and at the same level or hip-width apart with the stronger foot slightly lower in the water. In both cases the feet are placed just under the water surface.

TAKE YOUR MARKS   The swimmer bends the elbows and pulls the body upwards and inwards. The back is rounded and the chest is brought close to the knees. The knees break the water surface between the bent arms and the swimmer will be looking downwards and towards the wall. The hips are just below the water surface at this phase of the start.

STARTING SIGNAL   The swimmer presses downwards, lifts the hips clear of the water surface and the body upwards and away from the block. The head is moved upwards and backwards, the straight arms are brought sideways and backwards in a vigorous swinging action and the legs are extended explosively. Some swimmers bring the arms over bent and then stretch but, if incorrectly performed, this can lead to unnecessary height. With the final ankle extension the swimmer extends and slightly arches the back, looks upwards and outwards and encloses the head between the outstretched arms. The swimmer inhales during the early part of this release stage.

FLIGHT   The swimmer stretches from the fingertips to the toes with the head held back and between the arms. The slight arch is maintained and the hands are brought together in preparation for a streamlined entry. The swimmer concentrates on getting outwards and keeps this back dive as low as possible.

ENTRY   The swimmer enters through the fingertips with the head back and the hips up. The arms must be fully stretched with the hands close together and the fingers in line with the arms. The entry causes the minimum of splash and is made at a very narrow angle to the water surface.

GLIDE, PULL AND SURFACE   The glide is made in a streamlined position with the head in line with the rest of the body. The arch is not maintained during the glide and the body is kept beneath the water surface as near as possible to the horizontal. The swimmer exhales mainly through the nose during this underwater phase of the start. After a short glide the swimmer reaches swimming speed and kicks and pulls with one arm. The head is brought forwards and breaks the water surface as the pulling arm is about to recover and the arm extended beyond the head is about to pull.

More recently some swimmers have been using a dolphin leg kick after the glide, so delaying the pull and break to the water surface.

TEACHING POINTS – BACKSTROKE START

Starting position
a) grasp the handholds (trough or rail)
b) grasp shoulder-width apart
c) keep the arms straight
d) place the feet against the wall
e) place the feet hip-width apart
f) place the feet just under the surface
g) place the feet at the same level

or

place one foot slightly higher

Take your marks
a) bend the elbows
b) pull the body upwards
c) pull the body upwards and to the wall
d) lift the trunk out of the water
e) round the back
f) bring the chest close to the knees
g) keep the knees between the arms
h) look at the block

Starting signal

a) press downwards
b) lift the body upwards
c) swing the arms sideways
   and backwards
d) swing and breathe in
e) move the head upwards
   and backwards
f) lift the hips
g) explode upwards and
   backwards
h) straighten the legs
i) push with the toes
j) drive outwards

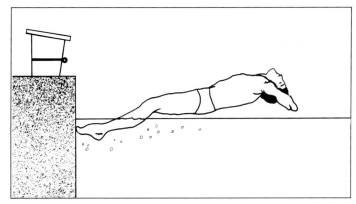

Flight

a) stretch over the surface
b) stretch from the fingertips
   to the toes
c) stretch the arms above the
   head
d) hold the hands together
e) squash the ears
f) keep the head back and
   between the arms

Entry

a) enter through the fingertips
b) stretch the fingers
c) keep the head back
d) keep the hips up

Glide, pull and surface

a) sink and stretch
b) stretch and glide
c) glide and bring the head
   forwards
d) glide and breathe out
e) breathe out under water
f) breathe out through the
   nose
g) glide briefly
h) glide, kick and pull with
   one arm
i) kick and pull with one arm
j) keep one arm above the
   head
k) pull to the surface
l) stretch for the surface

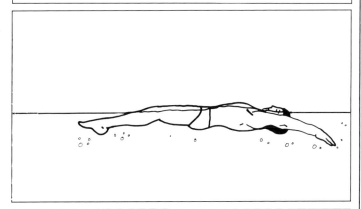

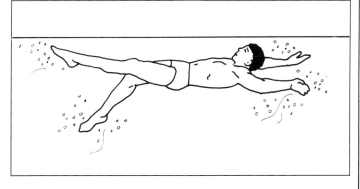

Breaststroke and butterfly open turns

APPROACH The swimmer touches the wall with both hands together and, in butterfly, at the same level. The touch is made with the shoulders square and just as the arm recovery is completed. The head and shoulders are kept low.

TURN The swimmer bends the arms on contact and starts to tuck the legs. The swimmer looks in the direction of the turn and turns the upper body on to the side. As the bottom arm is released and moved away from the wall beneath the surface and close to the chest, the tucked legs are pulled under the body and towards the wall. During the early part of the turn the swimmer inhales. The top arm pushes the upper body away from the wall and is then released and taken over the water surface.

SINK The swimmer sinks on the side and the arm that is released over the water surface enters partially bent and beyond the head. Meanwhile the first released arm has been brought forward beneath the water surface to a similar position. With both hands beneath the water surface, the feet are placed sideways on the wall at a depth of thirty to forty centimetres for butterflyers and sixty to seventy centimetres for breaststrokers. The hands are pushed forwards and towards each other as the upper body starts to twist on to the front.

PUSH The head is kept down between the arms as the swimmer, from a semi-crouch position, thrusts against the wall. The swimmer moves into the prone position with the shoulders level before the final ankle extension is made. The swimmer leaves the wall in a fully stretched position.

GLIDE, PULL AND SURFACE The swimmer looks downwards and keeps the head in line with the stretched body and limbs. The streamlined position is maintained until the swimmer slows down to swimming speed. In the butterfly-stroke there is a brief glide followed by an upward kick, the swimmer then kicks down and starts to pull with the arms. Prior to breaking the water surface the swimmer exhales through the mouth and nose and starts to raise the head in preparation for the inhalation. The swimmer pushes the chin forwards and inhalation is made as the pull is completed. Some swimmers delay the exhalation and pull twice before raising the head to inhale. In the breaststroke it takes longer to slow down to swimming speed than in the butterfly-stroke and, therefore, the glide is held for a longer time. The swimmer then pulls either outwards, backwards and inwards with straight arms, or starts pulling in a sideways direction with straight arms, bends and keeps the elbows high, moves the hands close together and finally extends the arms. In both cases the hands finish close to the thighs and remain there for about one and a half seconds as a streamlined body position is maintained. The hands are then recovered near to the chest with the elbows being kept close to the trunk, and as the arms pass the chest the legs start to recover. With the arms nearly straight the kick backwards is made and the head starts to rise to angle the body towards the surface. With the arms fully stretched and the legs almost together the top of the head breaks the water surface. The second arm pull out of the turn must not start until the head breaks the surface. During the latter part of the underwater sequence the swimmer exhales and is ready to inhale at the end of the second arm pull.

TEACHING POINTS – BREASTSTROKE OPEN (or UPRIGHT) TURN

Approach

a) touch the wall with both hands together
b) touch on the front
c) keep the head low

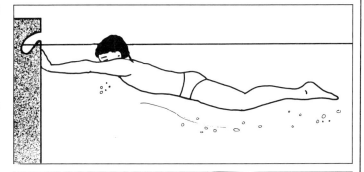

Turn

a) bend the arms on contact
b) tuck the legs and bend the arms
c) tuck the legs tightly
d) look in the direction of the turn
e) push the body to one side
f) turn the upper body on the side
g) turn and release the outside arm
h) pull the feet under the body
i) move the trunk up and over
j) keep the shoulders low
k) turn and breathe in

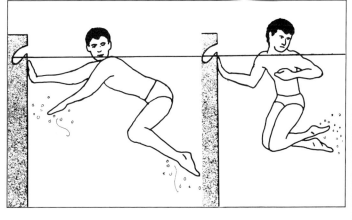

l)   move the outside arm in
     the new directon
m) release the inside arm over
     the surface (more
     advanced swimmer)

or

place the hand in the water
immediately
n)   release and plant the feet

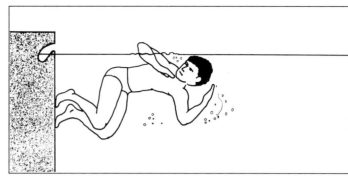

Sink

a) sink on the side
b) sink and move both hands
   to the head
c) bring the hands together
   above the head
d) sink and twist on to the front
e) twist and stretch the arms

Push

a) stretch and thrust with the
   legs
b) stretch from the fingertips
   to the toes
c) keep the head down
   between the arms
d) push away on the front
e) push slightly downwards

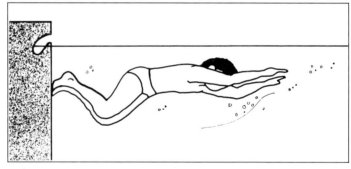

Glide, pull and surface

a) stretch and glide
b) glide and then pull to the
    thighs
c)   **either**
    i) pull outwards and to the
       side
    ii) keep the arms straight

or

    i) pull outwards and
       backwards
    ii) bend and stretch the
        arms

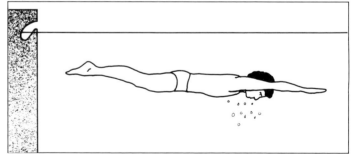

d) glide, pull, glide
e) pull with the head down
f) pull, glide and recover
g) recover the arms and legs
h) recover the arms close to
   the body

i) bring the arms upwards
    close to the chest
j) stretch the arms and kick
k) kick and stretch to the
    surface
l) kick and lift the head

m) stretch the arms and lift
   the head
n) stretch to the surface
o) break the surface with the
   head

TEACHING POINTS – BUTTERFLY OPEN (or UPRIGHT) TURN

Approach

a) touch the wall with both hands level and together
b) touch on the front
c) keep the head low

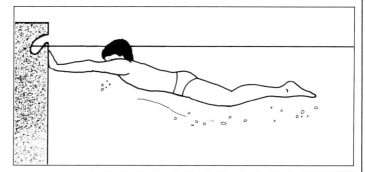

Turn

a) bend the arms on contact
b) tuck the legs and bend the arms
c) tuck the legs tightly
d) look in the direction of the turn
e) push the body to one side
f) turn the upper body on the side
g) turn and release the outside arm
h) pull the feet under the body
i) move the trunk up and over
j) keep the shoulders low
k) turn and breathe in
l) move the outside arm in the new direction
m) release the inside arm over the surface (more advanced swimmer)

or

place the hand in the water immediately
n) release and plant the feet

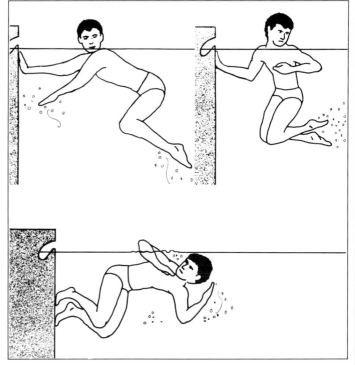

Sink

a) sink on the side
b) sink and move both hands to the head
c) bring the hands together above the head
d) sink and twist on to the front
e) twist and stretch the arms

Push

a) stretch and thrust with the legs
b) stretch from the fingertips to the toes

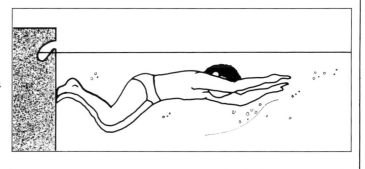

c) keep the head down
   between the arms
d) push away on the front

Glide, pull and surface
a) stretch and glide
b) glide briefly
c) glide and bring the feet up
d) kick down and pull
e) kick and look forwards and
   upwards
f) glide, kick and pull to the
   surface
g) breathe out underwater
h) breathe out through the

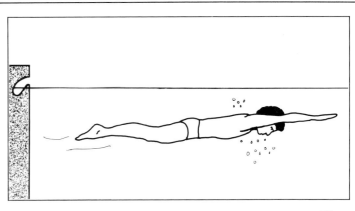

                                                    or

mouth and nose   pull twice and then breathe
i) pull and then breathe in   in

Lateral spin turns: head out and head under (frontcrawl)

APPROACH   The swimmer stretches the leading arm towards the pool side and touches with the palm of the hand flat against the wall just below the water surface. The fingers are placed so that they are pointing inwards and in the direction of the turn. In the head out turn the swimmer looks along the water surface and in the head under turn the swimmer looks downwards. In both turns the other arm is kept by the side of the body.

TURN   The swimmer bends the leading arm on contact, turns the head away from the touching arm and tucks the legs. In the head out turn the body is brought from a horizontal to a near upright position and the swimmer has no difficulty breathing in as the mouth clears the water surface. In the head under turn the trunk is kept horizontal and the inhalation can be made by turning the face sideways as the head starts to move away from the wall. In both turns the spin is created by the contact hand being pressed against the wall and the arm straightening. The trailing arm in the head under turn is pushed outwards from the hips to the head to aid the turn, whereas the trailing arm performs more of a sculling action in the head out turn and helps in balancing the near upright position as well as aiding the turn. In both turns the knees are kept close together and the tuck maintained throughout. As the feet move towards the wall the swimmer starts to move the arms to a bent position in front of the head. In the head out turn the swimmer has to plunge the head and shoulders downwards to place the trunk in a horizontal position, but in the head under turn a slight downwards movement of the head is sufficient.

PUSH The feet are placed firmly against the wall at a depth of thirty to forty centimetres, and, from a semi-crouched position, the swimmer extends the arms and pushes vigorously with the legs. The head is kept down between the outstretched arms as the swimmer stretches from the fingertips to the toes. As the swimmer moves into the glide position exhalation starts through the mouth and nose.

GLIDE, PULL AND SURFACE The swimmer points the fingers forwards and slightly upwards and holds a brief glide. Exhalation continues as the swimmer kicks and pulls with one arm to break the water surface. The head is raised slightly as the swimmer turns to inhale. Some swimmers pull once with each arm before taking the first inhalation but this depends upon the individual.

TEACHING POINTS – LATERAL SPIN TURN: head out

Approach

a) stretch the leading arm towards the wall

b) reach in front of the head

c) touch the wall with the palm of the hand flat

d) touch with the fingers pointing in the direction of the turn

e) touch with the fingers pointing inwards

f) touch the wall under the surface

g) keep the trailing arm by the side

h) look along the surface

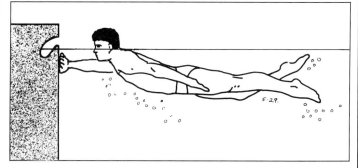

Turn

a) bend the leading arm on contact

b) bend the leading arm and tuck the legs

c) turn the head in the direction of the turn

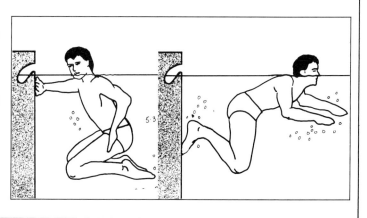

d) turn the head to the side of the trailing arm
e) lift the mouth clear of the surface
f) breathe in as the mouth clears the surface
g) turn by straightening the touching arm
h) turn the head and shoulders and move the feet towards the wall
i) release the leading arm before the feet touch the wall
j) release the leading arm and keep it close to the body
k) spin on the chest with the head up
l) spin and move both arms to a bent position beyond the head
m) spin and move both hands to the head
n) spin with the head up
o) spin with the legs tucked up
p) spin with the chest facing downwards

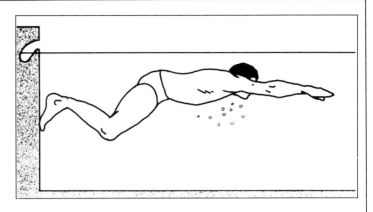

Sink
a) spin and then sink
b) spin and move the head down between the arms

Push
a) stretch the arms and push with the legs
b) straighten the legs and arms
c) push and stretch from the fingertips to the toes
d) keep the head down between the arms

Glide, pull and surface
a) stretch and glide
b) glide briefly
c) point the fingers forwards and upwards
d) kick and pull together
e) glide, kick and pull with one arm
f) kick and pull to the surface
g) pull and raise the head
h) breathe out underwater
i) breathe out through the mouth and nose
j) look to the side and breathe in
k) pull once and breathe in

or

pull twice and breathe in

TEACHING POINTS – LATERAL SPIN (CLOSED or FLAT) TURN: head under
Approach
a) stretch the leading arm towards the wall
b) touch the wall with the palm of the hand flat
c) touch with the fingers pointing in the direction of the turn
d) touch with the fingers pointing inwards
e) touch the wall under the surface
f) keep the head and shoulders down

Turn

a) bend the leading arm on contact
b) bend the leading arm and tuck the legs
c) turn the head in the direction of the turn
d) turn the face sideways to breathe
e) turn the upper body in the opposite direction to the touching arm
f) turn by straightening the touching arm
g) turn the head and the shoulders and move the feet towards the wall
h) release the leading arm before touching the wall with the feet
i) release the leading arm and keep it close to the body
j) spin on the chest with the head down
k) spin and move both arms to a bent position beyond the head
l) spin and move both hands to the head
m) spin with the legs tucked up
n) spin with the chest facing downwards
o) lift the head and the shoulders slightly upwards during the spin
p) look ahead

Sink

a) spin and sink

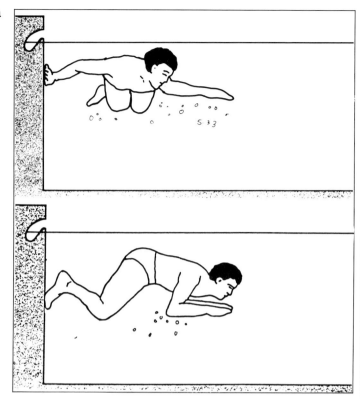

b) move the head down between the arms

Push

a) stretch the arms and push with the legs
b) straighten the legs and arms
c) push and stretch from the fingertips to the toes
d) keep the head down between the arms

Glide, pull and surface

a) stretch and glide
b) glide briefly

c) point the fingers forwards and upwards
d) kick and pull together
e) glide, kick and pull with one arm
f) kick and pull to the surface
g) pull and raise the head
h) breathe out underwater
i) breathe out through the mouth and nose
j) look to the side and breathe in
k) pull once and breathe in

or

pull twice and breathe in

Throw-away turn (frontcrawl)

APPROACH   The swimmer stretches the leading arm towards the pool side and rolls on to that side. The palm of the hand is placed flat against the wall with the fingers pointing upwards. In the early stages of learning the turn it is probably easier to take hold of the rail or trough.

TURN
The swimmer bends the leading arm on contact, turns the head away from the touching arm and tucks the legs. The contact arm presses against the wall and the straightening arm turns the body on to the side in the opposite direction. The tucked legs swing towards the wall as the head moves up and just over the water surface. The trailing arm is taken away from the side of the body and is moved in the new direction. The swimmer inhales as the head comes up and over the water surface.

SINK
The contact arm is released and the hand is plunged into the water just beyond the head as the swimmer submerges on the side. The feet are placed in a sideways position thirty to forty centimetres below the water surface and the body sinks on the side to a similar depth. The arms are brought together in a partially bent position beyond the head.

PUSH
From a semi-crouch position the swimmer extends the arms and drives with the legs. The head is kept in line with the body and between the arms. The swimmer leaves the wall in a sideways position and stretched from the fingertips to the toes.

GLIDE, PULL AND SURFACE
The swimmer glides briefly, rolls on to the front and points the fingers forwards and slightly upwards, and then kicks and pulls to break the water surface. Exhalation takes place through the mouth and nose during this phase. The head is raised slightly on surfacing and the swimmer turns to inhale. Some swimmers pull once with each arm before taking the first inhalation but this depends upon the individual.

TEACHING POINTS – THROW-AWAY (GRAB, HEAD-OUT, UPRIGHT, PULL-UP or OPEN) TURN

Approach
a) roll on to the side of the leading arm
b) stretch the leading arm towards the wall
c) touch the wall with the palm of the hand flat
d) touch the wall with the fingers pointing upwards

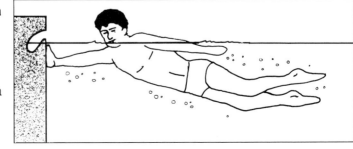

(ABOVE) *THROW-AWAY TURN:*
roll on to the side of the leading
arm.

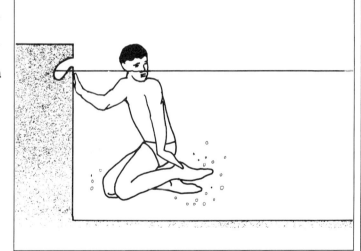

Turn

a) bend the leading arm on
   contact
b) tuck the legs and bend the
   leading arm
c) turn the upper body in the
   opposite direction to the
   touching arm
d) turn away from the
   touching arm
e) turn by straightening the
   touching arm
f) swing the tucked legs
   under and towards the wall
g) turn the upper body away
   from the wall
h) swing the tucked legs
   towards the wall
i) move the trunk up and
   over
j) swing the tucked legs
   inwards and the head
   away
k) keep the head just above
   the surface
l) breathe in as head moves
   up and over
m) keep the hand of the
   trailing arm near to the
   hips
n) turn the palm of the trailing
   hand downwards
o) turn the body on to the side
   and move the head up and
   over

Sink

a) sink the body on the side
b) turn to the side and sink
c) release and plunge the hand of the bent touching arm into the water
d) plunge the hand into the water above the head
e) plunge the bent touching arm into the water and sink
f) bring both arms close together above the head
g) move both hands to the head
h) sink with bent arms and legs
i) release the leading arm before planting the feet

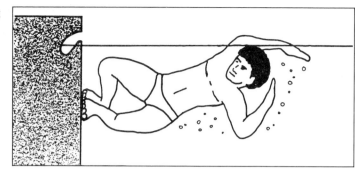

Push

a) stretch the arms and push with the legs
b) stay on the side and stretch the arms and legs
c) stretch on the side and thrust with the legs
d) drive and stretch from the fingertips to the toes
e) keep the head down between the arms

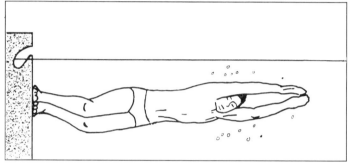

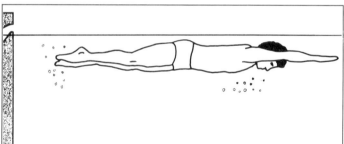

Glide, pull and surface

a) glide and roll on to the front
b) stretch and glide
c) glide briefly
d) point the fingers forwards and upwards
e) kick and pull together
f) glide, kick and pull with one arm
g) kick and pull to the surface
h) pull and raise the head
i) breathe out underwater
j) breathe out through the mouth and nose
k) look to the side and breathe in
l) pull once and breathe in

or

pull twice and breathe in

Twist and somersault turn (frontcrawl)

APPROACH The swimmer stretches the leading arm towards the pool side and rolls on to that side. The hand is placed beneath the water surface with the palm flat against the wall and the fingers pointing in the direction of the turn. The trailing arm is kept by the side of the body.

TURN   The swimmer bends the leading arm on contact, looks for the wall and twists on to the back. As the leading arm bends, the head is taken backwards and the legs are tucked. The contact arm is now straightened, and the head and shoulders are turned in the opposite direction. The knees are brought upwards and slightly to one side and then taken over the water surface. With the release of the contact hand the swimmer completes a tucked half-somersault. As the feet hit the wall at a depth of thirty to forty centimetres the hands, having been brought upwards and near to the body, will be close together below the face.

PUSH   From a semi-crouch position the swimmer extends the arms and drives with the legs. The head is kept in line with the body and between the arms. The swimmer leaves the wall on the front and stretches from fingertips to toes.

GLIDE, PULL AND SURFACE   The swimmer glides briefly with the fingers pointing forwards and slightly upwards, and then kicks and pulls to break the water surface. Exhalation will have taken place through the mouth and nose during this phase. The head will be raised slightly on surfacing, and the swimmer turns to inhale. Some swimmers pull once with each arm before taking the first inhalation but this depends upon the individual.

TEACHING POINTS – TWIST AND SOMERSAULT (or BACKWARD TUMBLE) TURN

Approach

a) roll on to the side of the leading arm
b) roll and stretch the leading arm towards the wall
c) breathe in and stretch for the wall
d) touch the wall with the palm of the hand flat
e) touch with the fingers pointing downwards and inwards
f) touch the wall under the surface
g) keep the trailing arm by the side of the body

Turn

a) bend the leading arm on contact

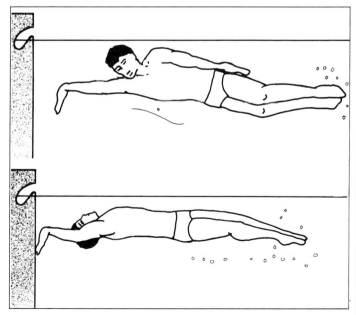

b) bend the touching arm and look at the wall

c) look for the wall and twist on to the back

d) tuck the legs as the leading arm bends

e) bring the knees up and over

f) tuck and somersault

g) turn the upper body in the opposite direction

h) somersault by straightening the leading arm against the wall

i) move the head and the shoulders in the opposite direction

j) move the feet towards the wall

k) tuck the legs and throw them over the surface

l) throw the legs over the surface and to one side

m) move the trailing hand to a bent position near the head

n) move the trailing arm close to the body

o) bring the touching arm to a bent position near the head

p) move the feet to the wall and the hands to the head

q) move both hands to a bent position near the head

r) move both hands upwards and close to the body

s) move both hands to the head

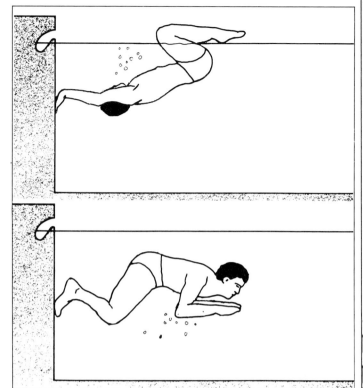

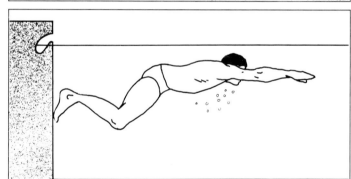

Push

a) stretch the arms and thrust with the legs

b) stretch and thrust with the legs

c) thrust and keep the head down

d) keep the head down between the arms

e) straighten the legs and the arms

f) thrust and stretch from the fingertips to the toes

g) push away on the front

Glide, pull and surface

a) stretch and glide

b) glide briefly

c) point the fingers forwards and upwards

d) kick and pull together

e) glide, kick and pull with one arm

f) kick and pull to the surface

g) pull and raise the head

h) breathe out underwater

i) breathe out through the mouth and nose

j) look to the side and breathe in

k) pull once and breathe in

or

pull twice and breathe in

Forward tumble turn (frontcrawl)

APPROACH
The swimmer approaches at speed, takes an inhalation and looks forward in preparation for the turn. The trailing arm remains at the side of the body and the leading arm is pulled to a similar position. Both palms are turned downwards and the legs bend slightly at the hips and knees.

TURN
The swimmer drops the head and shoulders and kicks and pushes downwards when just over a metre from the wall. As the hips come over the water surface, the head starts to move in the opposite direction. The swimmer performs a circular action with one hand and twists the body to that side. With the other hand the swimmer continues pulling towards the head. As the legs are thrown over the water surface they are tucked, and the body, aided by the circling arm continues on to the side. The feet are placed sideways on the wall and the hands are brought together just beyond the head.

PUSH
From a semi-crouch position the swimmer starts to straighten the arms and commences the leg thrust. The final push is made with the head down between the extended arms. The swimmer leaves the wall stretching from the fingertips to the toes and in the prone position with the shoulders nearly level.

GLIDE, PULL AND SURFACE
The glide is made in a streamlined position with the head in line with the rest of the body. After a short glide the swimmer kicks and pulls with one arm, and raises the head slightly forwards. The swimmer's head breaks the water surface as the pulling arm is about to recover and the arm extended beyond the head is about to pull. The swimmer exhales through the mouth and nose during the glide-pull phase and, by raising the head slightly, is ready to inhale on surfacing. Some swimmers delay the exhalation and inhale after the second arm pull has been made.

TEACHING POINTS – FORWARD TUMBLE (FLIP or SOMERSAULT) TURN

Approach
a) look forwards to the wall
b) pull the leading arm back to the side
c) keep the trailing arm at the side of the body
d) turn the palms downwards
e) keep the legs together and bend the knees

Turn

a) pull the head and shoulders downwards

b) pull the head backwards and downwards

c) push the palms and the feet downwards

d) drop the head and kick downwards

e) kick downwards and force the hips upwards

f) force the hips upwards and forwards

g) pull one hand towards the head

h) scull inwards with one hand

i) move the head away from the wall

j) move the hips to the wall

k) force the seat upwards and to one side

m) pike the body and then tuck the legs

n) pike and tuck loosely

o) turn the head and the shoulders on to the side of the sculling arm

p) tumble and twist on to the side

q) tuck the legs and twist the head and shoulders

r) place the feet sideways on the wall

s) hit the wall on the side

t) hit the wall and move the hands beyond the head

u) move both arms to a bent position beyond the head

v) bring the hands together beyond the head

w) keep the head down between the arms

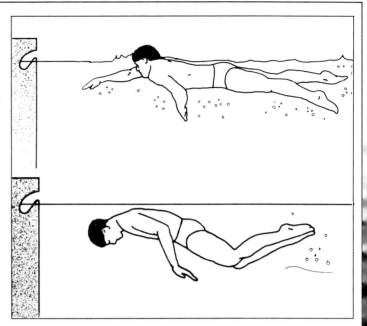

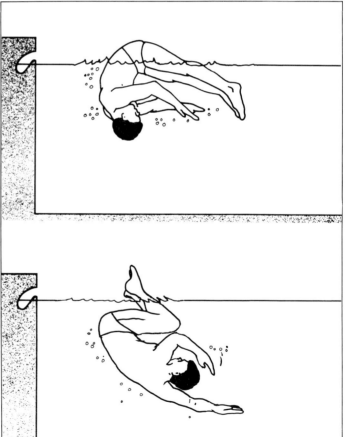

Push

a) straighten the arms and thrust with the legs

b) straighten the arms and the legs

(ABOVE) *FORWARD TUMBLE TURN:* hit the wall and move the hands beyond the head.

c) push with the ankles and turn on to the front
d) thrust and move on to the front
e) move on to the chest during the thrust outwards

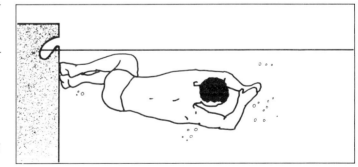

Glide, pull and surface

a) stretch and glide
b) glide briefly
c) point the fingers forwards and upwards
d) kick and pull together
e) glide, kick and pull with one arm
f) kick and pull to the surface
g) pull and raise the head
h) breathe out underwater
i) breathe out through the mouth and nose
j) look to the side and breathe in
k) pull once and breathe in
or
pull twice and breathe in

Backcrawl spin turns: head out and head under

APPROACH In both turns the swimmer stretches the leading arm towards the wall and touches with the palm flat against the wall. In the head out turn the swimmer touches just below the water surface and points the fingers in the direction of the turn, and in the head under turn the touch is twenty-five to thirty centimetres below the water surface and the fingers are pointed downwards and towards the centre line. In the head out turn the head is kept forward with the chin in, and in the head under turn the head is kept back and just beneath the water surface. In both turns the other arm is kept at the side and the legs kick hard into the turn.

TURN With both turns the swimmer comes close to the wall by bending the contact arm. In the head out turn the legs are tucked and the swimmer spins on the back with the legs mainly below the water surface. In the head under turn the knees are thrust upwards and the lower legs and knees are lifted clear of the water surface: the legs are then thrown sideways and towards the contact arm. In the head under turn the swimmer should keep the upper body and head just below the water surface and should think of the turn as a spinning movement on the back with the lower legs and the knees remaining above the water surface. In both turns, the spin is created by the contact hand being pressed against the wall and the arm straightening and by the trailing hand performing a sculling action. The legs are kept close together during the spin and the tuck is maintained. As the feet are moved towards the wall the arms are moved to a bent position beyond the head with the palms facing upwards. In the head out turn the swimmer submerges the head and upper body as the arms move upwards.

PUSH The feet are whipped round and hit the wall at a depth of thirty to forty centimetres. From a semi-crouch position the swimmer extends the arms and pushes with the legs. The swimmer stretches from the fingertips to the toes as the final push from the toes is made. From this point the swimmer starts to exhale through the mouth and nose, but mainly through the nose.

GLIDE, PULL AND SURFACE The glide is made in a streamlined position with the head in line with the rest of the body. After a short glide the swimmer reaches swimming speed and kicks and pulls with one arm. The head is brought forwards and breaks the water surface as the pulling arm is about to recover and the arm extended beyond the head is about to pull.

TEACHING POINTS – BACKCRAWL SPIN TURN: *head out*

Approach

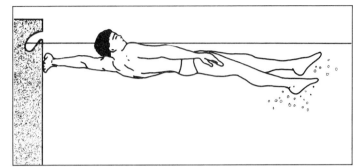

a) stretch the leading arm towards the wall
b) breathe in and stretch for the wall
c) touch the wall with the palm of the hand flat
d) point the fingers in the direction of the turn
e) point the fingers inwards
f) touch the wall under the surface
g) keep the chin in
h) hold the trailing arm by the side

Turn

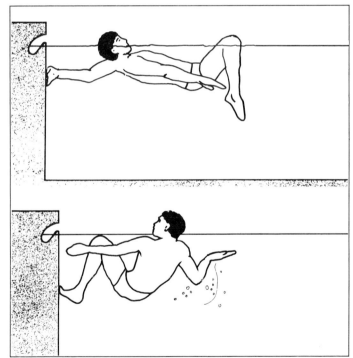

a) bend the leading arm on contact
b) tuck the legs and bend the leading arm
c) tuck and follow the leading arm
d) turn the head in the direction of the turn
e) turn the upper body in the new direction
f) straighten the leading arm against the wall
g) push and straighten the leading arm
h) swing the tucked legs to the wall
i) spin the body with the chest facing upwards
j) spin with the head forwards
k) spin on the back
l) spin with the legs tucked
m) keep the knees close together

n) release the leading arm and spin
o) move both arms to a bent position above the head
p) move the hands with the palms facing upwards

Sink

a) spin and sink
b) sink the upper body
c) sink and bring the hands to the head
d) sink and place the feet on the wall

e) move the head back
between the arms

Push

a) straighten the arms and
push with the legs
b) stretch the arms and the
legs
c) drive and stretch from the
fingertips to the toes
d) keep the head between the
arms

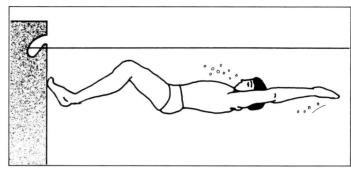

Glide, pull and surface

a) glide and stretch
b) glide and bring the head
forwards
c) glide and breathe out
d) breathe out under water
e) breathe out through the
nose
f) glide briefly
g) glide, kick and pull with
one arm
h) kick and pull with one arm

i) kick and pull
j) keep one arm above the
head

k) pull to the surface
l) stretch for the surface

TEACHING POINTS – BACKCRAWL SPIN (FLIP, WHIP or TUMBLE) TURN: *head under*

Approach

a) stretch the leading arm
towards the wall
b) breathe in and stretch for
the wall
c) stretch the arm and look
back
d) keep the head back
e) touch the wall with the palm
of the hand flat
f) point the fingers
downwards and inwards
g) touch the wall under the
surface
h) reach downwards and in
front of the head
i) hold the trailing arm by the
side

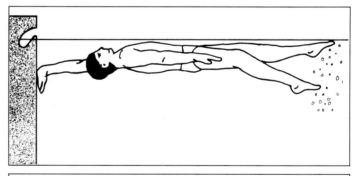

Turn

a) bend the leading arm on
contact

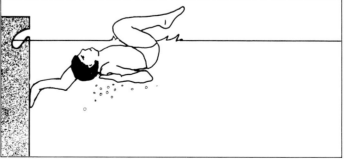

b) tuck the legs and bend the leading arm

c) thrust the knees upwards

d) lift and throw the legs sideways over the surface

e) throw the legs sideways towards the contact arm

f) keep the knees close together

g) push the body round with the leading arm

h) push and straighten the leading arm

i) pull the trailing arm upwards

j) pull the trailing hand towards the head

k) turn the body with the chest facing upwards

l) keep flat on the back

m) turn and bring the hands to the head

n) bring the hands together above the head

o) plant the feet and bring the hands together

Push

a) straighten the arms and push with the legs

b) stretch the arms and legs

c) drive and stretch from the fingertips to the toes

d) keep the head between the arms

Glide, pull and surface

a) glide and stretch

b) glide and bring the head forwards

c) glide and breathe out

d) breathe out under water

e) breathe out through the nose

f) glide briefly

g) glide, kick and pull with one arm

h) kick and pull with one arm

i) kick and pull

j) keep one arm above the head

k) pull to the surface

l) stretch for the surface

6 STARTING AND TURNING PRACTICES

Starting practices:
front start

1. Subject practises plunge dives from the pool side.

2. Subject practises plunge dives from the pool side followed by a long glide.

3. Subject practises plunge dives from the pool side followed by long glides at varying depths.

4. Subject practises plunge dives from the pool side followed by different length glides.

5. Subject practises plunge dives from the pool side followed by different length glides at varying depths

6. Subject practises racing dives from the pool side using different arm movements. (See illustrations opposite.)

7. In the water and hold the pool side: the subject submerges, pushes away from the pool side and performs a long glide.

8. In the water and hold the pool side: the subject submerges, pushes away from the pool side and glides at varying depths.

9. In the water and hold the pool side: the subject submerges, pushes away from the pool side and performs either short glides close to the surface or long glides beneath the surface.

10. In the water and hold the pool side (frontcrawl and butterfly): the subject submerges, pushes away from the pool side, performs a short glide and kicks and pulls to the water surface. In the frontcrawl the pull is made with one arm and in the butterfly with two arms simultaneously.

11. In the water and hold the pool side (breaststroke): the

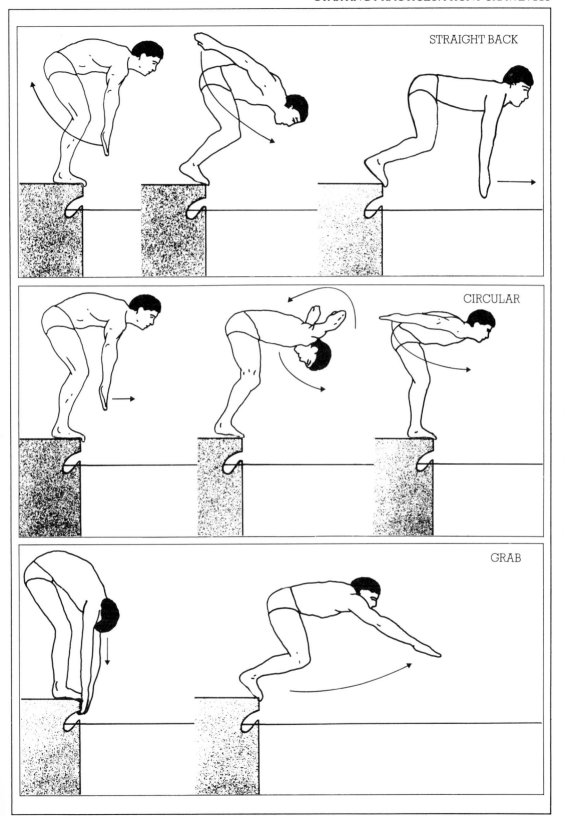

STRAIGHT BACK

CIRCULAR

GRAB

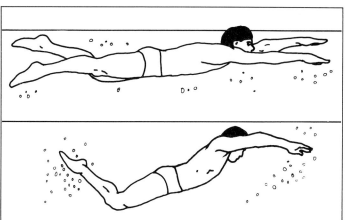

subject submerges, pushes away from the pool side, performs a long and deep glide (at a depth of about half a metre) pulls to the side with both arms and glides, and then kicks to the surface. The head must break the water surface in breaststroke before the next arm pull starts.

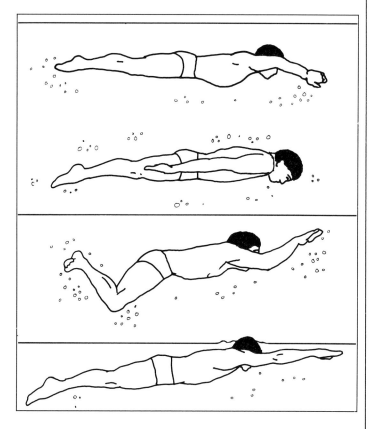

12. Subject practises racing dives from the pool side,

glides briefly near the water surface, kicks and pulls to the surface (butterfly and frontcrawl).

13. Subject practises racing dives from the pool side, glides for approximately two seconds at a depth of about half a metre, pulls and glides and then kicks to the water surface (breaststroke).

14. Subject practises racing dives from the pool side with either a partner or the teacher giving the correct starting commands (viz. *Take your marks – Go!*).

15. Subject practises racing dives from the pool side on the correct starting instructions and follows this up with the correct depths and stroke patterns.

16. Subject practises starts and racing dives from the pool side and competes over short distances on the three prone strokes.

17. Subject practises starts and racing dives from starting blocks.

Starting practices: backstroke start

1. Subject practises backstroke starts and glides just under the water surface.

2. Subject practises the push and glide movement and kicks and pulls with one arm to the water surface.

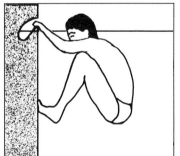 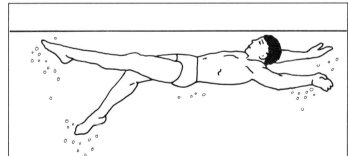

3. Subject practises backstroke starts, performs a short glide just under the water surface and kicks and pulls with one arm to the water surface.

4. Subject practises backstroke starts with either a partner or the teacher giving the correct starting command (viz. *Take your marks – Go!*).

5. Subject practises backstroke starts and competes over short distances.

Turning practices: breaststroke and butterfly open turns

1. Stand in chest-depth water three to four metres from the pool side: the subject swims to the pool side and touches the wall with both hands simultaneously.

2. Stand in chest-depth water three to four metres away from the pool side: the subject swims to the pool side, touches the wall with both hands simultaneously, turns, submerges and pushes off into a glide on the front.

3. Hold the pool side: in butterfly, the subject pushes and glides beneath the water surface and kicks and pulls to the water surface after a short, shallow glide. In breaststroke, the subject pulls after a long deep glide, holds a further glide and kicks and recovers the arms to break the water surface with the head.

4. Stand in chest-depth water three to four metres away from the pool side: the subject swims to the pool side, touches the wall with both hands simultaneously, turns and submerges. In butterfly, the subject kicks and pulls to the water surface after a short, shallow glide. In breast-stroke the subject pulls after a long deep glide, holds a further glide, and kicks and recovers the arms to break the water surface with the head.

5. Subject practises the turns at speed from push-offs in deep water, from racing dives and in competitive situations.

Turning practices: frontcrawl spin turns with head out and head under

1. Subject practises a mushroom float.

2. Hold the pool side: the subject pushes away from the pool side, glides and spins in a tucked position.

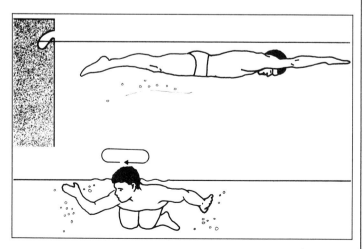

3. Stand in chest-depth water three to four metres away from the pool side: the subject swims slowly to the pool side, spins away from the touching arm with either the head up or down, and pushes and glides to the surface with the head between the arms.

4. Stand in chest-depth water three to four metres away from the pool side: the subject swims slowly to the pool side, spins away from the touching arm with either the head up or down, glides, and kicks and pulls with one arm to break the water surface.

5. Subject practises the turns at speed, from push-offs in deep water, from racing dives and in competitive situations.

Turning practices: frontcrawl throw-away turn

1. Hold the pool side: the subject submerges on the side and pushes away from the pool side.

2. Hold the pool side: the subject submerges on the side, pushes away from the pool side and glides on the front.

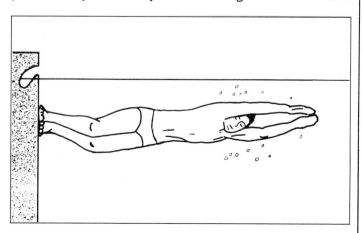

3. Hold the pool side: the subject submerges on the side, pushes away from the pool side, glides on the front and kicks and pulls with one arm to break the water surface.

4. Stand in chest-depth water three to four metres away from the pool side: the subject swims slowly to the pool side, turns away from the touching hand, submerges on the side and pushes and glides to the water surface on the front.

5. Stand in chest-depth water three to four metres away from the pool side: the subject swims slowly to the pool side, turns away from the touching hand, submerges on the side, glides, and kicks and pulls with one arm to break the water surface on the front.

6. Subject practises the turns at speed from push-offs in deep water, from racing dives and in competitive situations.

Turning practices: frontcrawl twist and somersault turn

1. Hold the pool side in deep water: push off on the back and perform a back tucked somersault.

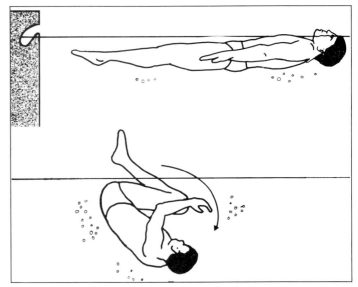

2. Hold the pool side in deep water: push off on the front, perform a half twist on to the back followed by a back somersault.

3. Either stand in the water up to the shoulders or tread water in the deep end three to four metres from the pool side: the subject swims to the pool side, performs a half

twist followed by a half somersault in the tucked position, pushes off from the side and glides to break the water surface.

4. Either stand in the water up to the shoulders or tread water in the deep end three to four metres from the pool side: the subject swims to the pool side, performs a half twist followed by a half somersault in the tucked position, pushes off from the side, glides, and kicks and pulls with one arm to break the water surface.

5. Subject practises the turns at speed from push-offs in deep water, from racing dives and in competitive situations.

Turning practices: frontcrawl tumble turn

1. Hold the pool side in deep water: the subject pushes from the pool side, performs several dolphin leg kicks while keeping the hands by the side, and then executes a forward tucked somersault.

2. Hold the pool side in deep water: the subject pushes from the pool side, performs several dolphin leg kicks while keeping the hands by the side, and then pushes downwards with the hands as the front tucked somersault is executed.

3. Hold the pool side in deep water: the subject pushes from the pool side, performs several dolphin leg kicks while keeping the hands by the side, pushes downwards with the hands, starts the somersault in a piked position and tucks late.

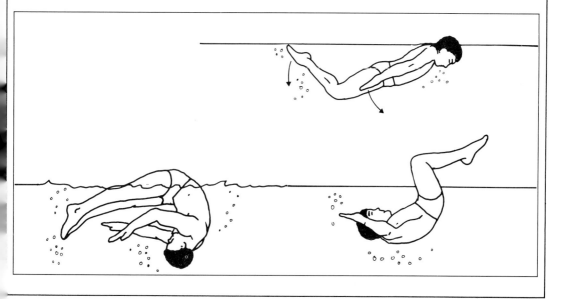

4. Either stand in water up to the shoulders or tread water in the deep end three to four metres from the pool side: the subject swims to the pool side, performs a somersault in a loose tuck position and pushes off on the back.

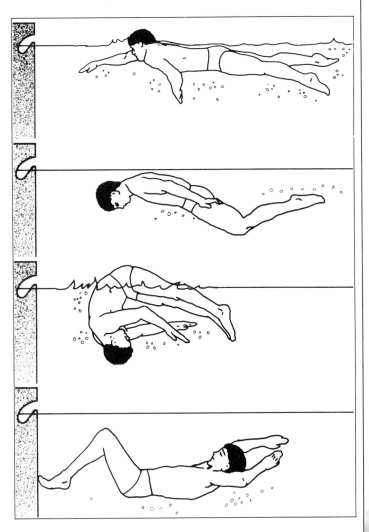

5. Hold the pool side in deep water: the subject pushes away from the pool side, swims several strokes, somersaults in a loose tuck position and twists on to the side.

6. Either stand in the water up to the shoulders or tread water in the deep end three to four metres from the pool side: the subject swims to the pool side, somersaults in a loose tuck position, performs a late twist, pushes off on the side and glides to break the water surface on the front.

7. Either stand in the water up to the shoulders or tread

water in the deep end three to four metres from the pool side: the subject swims to the pool side, performs a tumble turn, pushes off from the side, kicks and pulls with one arm to break the water surface.

8. Subject practises the turns at speed from push-offs in deep water, from racing dives and in competitive situations.

Turning practices: backcrawl spin turns with head out and head under

1. Stand in the shallow end: the subject practises spinning on the back with the legs tucked and the chin in.

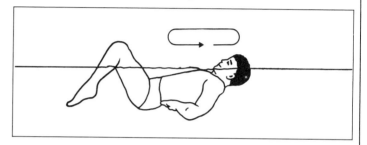

2. Hold on to the pool side: the subject pushes from the pool side on the back, glides and then spins on the back with the chin in.

3. Stand three to four metres from the pool side: the supine subject kicks to the pool side with one arm extended beyond the head, touches and spins on the back with the chin in.

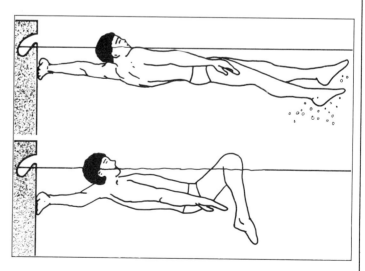

4. Hold on to the pool side: the subject submerges, pushes off on the back, glides and breathes out through the nose.

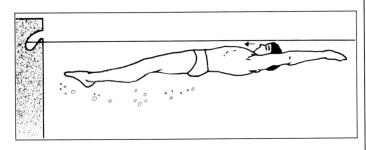

5. Hold on to the pool side: the subject submerges, pushes off on the back, glides, breathes out through the nose, and kicks and pulls with one arm to break the water surface.

6. Stand three to four metres from the pool side: the supine subject kicks to the pool side with one arm extended beyond the head, touches, spins on the back with the chin in, submerges, pushes off on the back, glides, breathes out through the nose, and kicks and pulls with one arm to break the water surface.

7. Stand three to four metres from the pool side: the supine subject swims backcrawl to the pool side, touches, spins on the back with the chin in, submerges, pushes off on the back, glides, breathes out through the nose and kicks and pulls with one arm to break the water surface.

8. Stand three to four metres from the pool side: the supine subject swims backcrawl to the pool side, brings the tucked legs up and round with the head back and under the water, pushes off on the back, glides, breathes out through the nose, and kicks and pulls with one arm to break the water surface.

9. Subject practises the turns at speed from push-offs, from backstroke starts and in competitive situations.

APPENDIX I – A SWIMMING PROGRAMME

The following swimming programme is an example of a four year plan for secondary school pupils. The course has been planned in a logical sequence and it is not meant to represent that of any particular school or institution. Pupils enter the secondary school with varying swimming abilities and backgrounds and it may be necessary to organize advanced and elementary courses for each year. It must be remembered that no one programme suits every individual and that within any one class a wide range of performance levels are found.

Although a time period (e.g. 6 weeks) is given for the teaching of new skills, each lesson also includes skills previously taught.

SWIMMING YEAR : I
LESSON TIME : 40 minutes
FREQUENCY : weekly
LENGTH OF
PROGRAMME : 36 weeks

Some basic skills and introduction to the strokes
6 weeks

i)   ways of getting the feet off the bottom of the bath and regaining the standing position
ii) rhythmic breathing, bobbing and floating
iii) body positions for glides and strokes
iv) leg kicks
v) arm actions
vi) co-ordination of arm and leg movements
Aids to be used if required

Crawl strokes   6 weeks

- i)   introduction to backcrawl
- ii) introduction to frontcrawl

Breaststroke and inverted breaststroke kick   6 weeks

- i)   introduction to breaststroke
- ii) introduction to inverted breaststroke kick

Other strokes   6 weeks

- i)   introduction to sidestroke
- ii) introduction to elementary backstroke

Some basic skills of survival   6 weeks

- i)   water entries, feet first and diving
- ii)   treading water
- iii) drownproofing
- iv)   submerging, feet first and head first
- v)   removal and inflation of clothing

Swimming rescues and expired air resuscitation
                                                     6 weeks

- i)   water safety
- ii)   reach, throw and wade
- iii) tow
- iv)   swim taking a support
- v)   swim and tow
- vi)   Expired air resuscitation techniques on land

SWIMMING YEAR : II
LESSON TIME : 40 minutes
FREQUENCY : weekly
LENGTH OF
PROGRAMME : 36 weeks

Elementary life saving   6 weeks

i)   identification of hazards, assessment of an emergency situation
ii) tows
iii) exits, landings and coma position
iv) expired air resuscitation techniques in water

Life saving awards   12 weeks

i) preparation for elementary life saving awards
ii) awards to be taken by pupils who satisfactorily complete the first part of this section

Improvement of crawl strokes and introduction to the butterfly stroke   6 weeks

i)   improvement of backcrawl
ii) improvement of frontcrawl
iii) introduction to the butterfly stroke

Improvement of breaststroke and inverted breaststroke kick   6 weeks

i) improvement of breaststroke
ii) improvement of inverted breaststroke kick

Elementary diving and racing starts   6 weeks

i)   early diving practices
ii) plunge dive and plain header
iii) forward pike and tuck dives
iv) forward racing start
v)   backstroke racing start

SWIMMING YEAR : III
LESSON TIME : 40 minutes
FREQUENCY : weekly
LENGTH OF
PROGRAMME : 36 weeks

Elementary personal survival   6 weeks

i)   swimming for speed and endurance
ii) swimming under water
iii) use of miscellaneous floats
iv) revision of water entries, treading water,
     drownproofing, submerging, removal and inflation
     of clothing and exits

Personal survival awards   6 weeks

i)   preparation for personal survival awards
ii) awards to be taken by pupils who satisfactorily
     complete the first part of this section

Other strokes   6 weeks

i)   improvement of sidestroke and elementary
     backstroke
ii) introduction to the trudgeon strokes

Starts and turns   6 weeks

i)   improvement of forward and backstroke racing
     starts
ii) introduction to open and tumble turns

Introduction to water polo   12 weeks

i)   water polo rules
ii) introduction to the skills of treading water, ball
     handling, dribbling, passing, catching and shooting
iii) introduction to team formations

SWIMMING YEAR : IV
LESSON TIME : 40 minutes
FREQUENCY : weekly
LENGTH OF
PROGRAMME : 36 weeks

Advanced swimming or diving 12 weeks

i) improvement of stroke technique
ii) improvement of starts and turns
iii) conditioning techniques
iv) competition
   or
i) revision of plain header and forward pike and tuck dives
ii) introduction to back dive, inward dive, forward dive half twist
iii) introduction to forward and backward somersaults
iv) improvement of dives introduced in sections (ii) and (iii)
v) using the springboard
vi) competition

NOTE: the choice depends upon teacher expertise, pupil competence and conditions.

Personal survival or life saving 12 weeks

Pupils elect to prepare for a more advanced award in either personal survival or life saving

i) preparation for more advanced personal survival or life saving awards
ii) awards to be taken by pupils who satisfactorily complete the first part of this section

Water polo 12 weeks

i) revision of water polo rules
ii) improvement of the skills concerned with treading water, ball handling, dribbling, passing, catching and shooting
iii) introduction to guarding
iv) introduction to team defence and offence

APPENDIX II – QUICK REFERENCE FOR MAIN TEACHING POINTS

The swimming strokes

BREASTSTROKE: MAIN TEACHING POINTS

Body position (prone and non-inhalation position)
a) look forwards and downwards

Legs (recovery)
STARTING POSITION:
the legs and the ankles are stretched and together
a) bring the heels up to the seat
b) cock and turn the feet outwards before the kick
c) keep the knees close together and high (advanced swimmer)

Legs (kick)
a) sweep the legs round and together
b) kick backwards and together (advanced swimmer)

Arms (pull)
STARTING POSITION:
the arms are stretched in front of the body (glide position)
a) pull outwards and downwards
b) keep the arms straight
c) press and bend (advanced swimmer)
d) keep the elbows up (advanced swimmer)

Arms (recovery)
a) bend the arms and bring the hands to the chin
b) stretch the arms forwards
c) swirl the hands together and forwards (advanced swimmer)

Breathing
a) breathe in during the pull
b) breathe out as the arms stretch forwards
c) breathe in at the end of the pull (advanced swimmer)

Timing
a) pull, recover, stretch and kick
b) thrust the arms forwards and then kick (advanced swimmer)

BACKCRAWL: MAIN TEACHING POINTS

Body position (supine)
a) look upwards

Legs
STARTING POSITION:
one leg is straight and near the surface and the other leg is bent with the foot at a depth of 30 to 45 centimetres
a) kick from the hips
b) stretch the toes

Arms (entry and pull)
STARTING POSITION:
one arm is straight and beyond the head
a) enter with the palm outwards
b) pull sideways with a straight arm
c) pull and push down the body (advanced swimmer)

Arms (recovery)
STARTING POSITION:
one arm is straight and by the side of the body
a) lift the hand up and back
b) keep the arm straight

Breathing
a) breathe in as one arm recovers and breathe out as the other arm recovers

Timing
a) kick and keep the arms moving

FRONTCRAWL: MAIN TEACHING POINTS

Body position (prone and non-inhalation position)
a) look downwards and slightly forwards

Legs
STARTING POSITION:
one leg is slightly bent and

near the water surface and the other leg is straight with the foot at a depth of approximately 30 centimetres
a) kick from the hips
b) point the toes

Arms (entry and pull)
STARTING POSITION:
one arm is almost straight and beyond the head
a) enter through the thumb
b) pull and keep the elbow up
c) push and straighten the arm

Arms (recovery)
STARTING POSITION:
one arm is almost straight by the side of the body
a) swing the elbow upwards and forwards
b) reach forwards with the hand

Breathing
a) breathe in as the hand on the breathing side completes the pull
b) breathe out when the face is submerged

Timing
a) kick and keep the arms moving

BUTTERFLY DOLPHIN: MAIN TEACHING POINTS

Body position (prone and non-inhalation position)
a) look downwards and slightly forwards

Legs
STARTING POSITION:
at the completion of the upbeat the legs are together, slightly bent with the toes pointed backwards;

at the completion of the downbeat the legs are together and straight with the ankles stretched
a) kick from the hips
b) kick up and down continuously
c) keep the legs together

Arms (entry and pull)
STARTING POSITION:
the arms are extended beyond the head and just wide of the shoulder line with the palms facing downwards and outwards
a) enter through the thumbs
b) pull and keep the elbows up
c) pull inwards and push backwards and outwards

Arms (recovery)
STARTING POSITION:
the arms are almost straight by the sides of the body with the elbows higher than the hands
a) swing the arms forwards in a low circular path
b) lower the face and recover the arms

Breathing
a) breathe in at the end of the pull
b) breathe out with increasing force during the pull

Timing
a) keep the legs moving during the arm action

SIDESTROKE: MAIN TEACHING POINTS

Body position (side)
a) lie on the side

Legs (recovery)
STARTING POSITION:
the legs and the ankles are stretched and together with the top leg resting on the bottom leg
a) bend and separate the legs
b) cock the top foot
c) point the toes of the bottom foot backwards

Legs (kick)
a) scissor and straighten the legs

Arms (pull and recovery)
STARTING POSITION:
the leading and bottom arm is stretched forwards, the top and trailing arm is stretched along the upper side of the body (side gliding position)
a) pull by bending the arm (bottom arm)
b) stretch the arm forwards beyond the head (bottom arm)
c) recover and bend the arm close to the body (top arm)
d) press the hand downwards and backwards (top arm)

Arms (timing)
a) bring the hands inwards
b) move the hands outwards

Breathing
a) bring the hands inwards and breathe in
b) breathe out and stretch the arms

Timing
a) bend the arms and legs

b) part the hands and kick

ELEMENTARY BACKSTROKE: MAIN TEACHING POINTS

Body position (supine)
a) look upwards

Whip kick legs (recovery)
STARTING POSITION:
the legs and the ankles are stretched and together just below the water surface
a) drop the heels downwards and backwards
b) cock and turn the feet outwards before the kick

Whip kick legs (kick)
a) sweep the lower legs round and together

Wedge kick legs (recovery)
STARTING POSITION:
the legs and the ankles are stretched and together just below the water surface
a) bend the legs and spread the knees
b) cock and turn the feet outwards before the kick

Wedge kick legs (kick)
a) straighten and bring the legs together

Arms (recovery)
STARTING POSITION:
the arms are straight at the side of the body in the glide position
a) slide the palms upwards along the body
b) stretch and make a 'V' shape beyond the head
c) keep the arms under the surface

Arms (pull)
a) sweep the arms round
b) pull with straight arms

Breathing
a) breathe in and recover the arms
b) breathe out and pull

Timing
a) recover the arms and legs
b) pull and kick

Elementary diving

PLAIN HEADER: MAIN TEACHING POINTS

Basic position
a) grip the toes round the edge of the pool
b) look forwards

Take-off
a) overbalance and drive the hips upwards
b) straighten the legs vigorously

Flight
a) maintain a slight bend at the hips
b) keep the limbs and body firm

Just prior to entry
a) close the arms

Entry
a) stretch from the fingertips to the toes

Submersion
a) sink and glide

Bottom of the pool reached
a) push upwards with the hands

Bottom of the pool not reached
a) direct the fingers upwards

Starts and turns

FRONT STARTS: MAIN TEACHING POINTS

Take your marks
a) place the feet hip-width apart
b) look forwards and downwards
c) grasp the front of the block (grab start)

Starting signal: circular backswing
a) circle the arms and drop

Starting signal: straight backswing
a) swing the arms backwards and forwards
b) swing the arms and drop

Starting signal: arms back
a) swing the arms upwards and backwards
b) swing the arms forwards and drop

Starting signal: grab start
a) pull downwards and forwards
b) swing the arms forwards

Flight
a) stretch and lower the head

Entry
a) stretch on entry

Glide, pull and surface: frontcrawl
a) glide, kick and pull with one arm

Glide, pull and surface: butterfly

a) glide, kick and pull to the surface

Glide, pull and surface: breaststroke

a) glide, pull, glide
b) kick and stretch to the surface

BACKSTROKE START: MAIN TEACHING POINTS

Starting position

a) place the feet hip-width apart

Take your marks

a) pull the body upwards and to the wall

Starting signal

a) explode upwards and backwards
b) swing the arms sideways and backwards

Flight

a) stretch over the surface
b) keep the head back and between the arms

Entry

a) enter through the fingertips

Glide, pull and surface

a) glide and bring the head forwards
b) kick and pull with one arm

BREASTSTROKE OPEN TURN: MAIN TEACHING POINTS

Approach

a) touch the wall with both hands together

Turn

a) tuck the legs tightly
b) turn the upper body on the side
c) release the inside arm over the surface

Sink

a) sink and move both hands to the head

Push

a) stretch and thrust with the legs
b) keep the head down between the arms

Glide, pull and surface

a) glide, pull, glide
b) kick and stretch to the surface

BUTTERFLY OPEN TURN: MAIN TEACHING POINTS

Approach

a) touch with both hands level and together

Turn

a) tuck the legs tightly
b) turn the upper body on the side
c) release the inside arm over the surface

Sink

a) sink and move both hands to the head

Push

a) stretch and thrust with the legs
b) keep the head down between the arms

Glide, pull and surface

a) glide, kick and pull to the surface

LATERAL SPIN TURN WITH HEAD OUT: MAIN TEACHING POINTS

Approach

a) touch with the fingers pointing inwards

Turn

a) spin on the chest with the head up
b) spin and move both hands to the head

Sink

a) spin and then sink

Push

a) stretch and thrust with the legs
b) keep the head down between the arms

Glide, pull and surface

a) glide, kick and pull with one arm

LATERAL SPIN TURN WITH HEAD UNDER: MAIN TEACHING POINTS

Approach

a) touch with the fingers pointing inwards

Turn

a) spin on the chest with the head down
b) spin and move both hands to the head
c) turn the face sideways to breathe

Sink

a) spin and sink

Push

a) stretch and thrust with the legs
b) keep the head down between the arms

Glide, pull and surface

a) glide, kick and pull with one arm

THROW-AWAY TURN: MAIN TEACHING POINTS

Approach
a) roll on to the side of the leading arm
b) touch with the hand flat and fingers pointing upwards

Turn
a) turn away from the touching arm
b) swing the tucked legs in and the head away

Sink
a) sink the body on the side
b) plunge the bent touching arm into the water and sink
c) move both hands to the head

Push
a) stretch on the side and thrust with the legs
b) keep the head down between the arms

Glide, pull and surface
a) glide and roll on to the front
b) glide, kick and pull with one arm

TWIST AND SOMERSAULT TURN: MAIN TEACHING POINTS

Approach
a) roll on to the side of the leading arm
b) touch with the fingers pointing downwards and inwards

Turn
a) bend the touching arm and look to the wall

b) tuck and somersault
c) move both hands to the head

Push
a) stretch and thrust with the legs
b) keep the head down between the arms

Glide, pull and surface
a) glide, kick and pull with one arm

FORWARD TUMBLE TURN: MAIN TEACHING POINTS

Approach
a) look forwards to the wall
b) pull the leading arm back to the side

Turn
a) pull the head downwards and backwards
b) force the hips upwards and forwards
c) tumble and twist on to the side

Push
a) stretch and thrust with the legs
b) thrust and move on to the front

Glide, pull and surface
a) stretch, kick and pull with one arm

BACKCRAWL SPIN TURN WITH HEAD OUT: MAIN TEACHING POINTS

Approach
a) touch with the hand flat
b) point the fingers inwards

Turn
a) tuck and follow the leading arm
b) spin on the back with the head forwards

Sink
a) sink and bring the hands to the head

Push
a) stretch and thrust with the legs
b) keep the head between the arms

Glide, pull and surface
a) glide and bring the head forwards
b) glide, kick and pull with one arm

BACKCRAWL SPIN TURN WITH HEAD UNDER: MAIN TEACHING POINTS

Approach
a) stretch the arm and look back
b) touch with the hand flat
c) point the fingers downwards and inwards

Turn
a) lift and throw the legs sideways over the surface
b) turn and bring the hands to the head

Push
a) stretch and thrust with the legs
b) keep the head between the arms

Glide, pull and surface
a) glide and bring the head forwards
b) glide, kick and pull with one arm